To Our Readers:

INTRODUCING

INTERNATIONAL

"The Book That Lies Flat"
— *User Friendly Binding* —

This title has been bound using state-of-the-art **OtaBind®** technology.

- The spine is 3-5 times stronger than conventional perfect binding
- The book lies open flat, regardless of the page being read
- The spine floats freely and remains crease-free even with repeated use

We are pleased to be able to bring this new technology to our customers.

Health Communications, Inc.

3201 S.W. 15th Street
Deerfield Beach, FL 33442-8190
(305) 360-0909

INTERNATIONAL

The Netherlands

Turning It Over

How to Find Tranquility When You Never Thought You Could

H.T.P.

Health Communications, Inc.
Deerfield Beach, Florida

Library of Congress Cataloging-in-Publication Data

H.T.P.
   Turning it over: finding tranquility when you never thought
you could / H.T.P.
      p.   cm.
   Includes bibliographical references.
   ISBN 1-55874-216-6
   1. Twelve-step programs — Religious aspects.   I. Title.
BJ1596.H16   1992   91-39667
158'.1—dc20   CIP

©1992 H.T.P.

ISBN 1-55874-216-6

Publisher: Health Communications, Inc.
              3201 S.W. 15th Street
              Deerfield Beach, Florida 33442-8190

Cover design by Barbara Bergman

 # Contents

Introduction

In His will is our peace.

Dante Alighieri

 In the shallows of an estuary, tiny fish hang motionless in a sunbeam outlined by the shadow of a mangrove branch. As the dark form of a larger fish looms into view, one of the small ones flashes into motion, then another, jiggling the kaleidoscopic pattern of liquid sunlight.

Overhead a tight formation of three pelicans glides gracefully above the surface. One of them peels off, dives and splashes awkwardly into the brownish green lagoon, soon surfacing with a fish tail frantically flapping from the side of its satchel beak.

As the pelican swallows convulsively, then heaves itself into the sky again, under the mangrove branch a tiny fish, motionless, peers from behind a sodden leaf and seems to tremble. It won't soon venture forth. All is quiet until the timeless stillness of this tranquil scene is interrupted again.

And again.

As I muse on this eternal interplay of life and death, my skiff drifting on the placid water near my South Florida home, I feel nostalgic. I sense my distant past. The mangrove roots that claw into the squishy black mud are my own. This is my world. I feel a part of it.

But how much a part of it am I really? For the pelicans and fish are acting on instinct — hunger and fear. To a great extent, I have freed myself, as have all of us, from the pull of instinct.

The birds and the fish are, if any creatures are, encompassed body and mind by their Creator's will. They have not the least awareness that their will and their lives are being directed by a Higher Power. But they are. They can will nothing and live in no way other than that which has been provided for them in nature, a creative force which some say springs from God.

Can the same be said of us?

Our will — is it truly our own? And can we do with it as we wish? Can we keep it or give it away? Is it our choice? Is it within our power?

Or are we driven willy-nilly by the same uncontrollable forces that cause the pelican to hurl itself into the water?

These are questions that sometimes nag me, and I know they trouble others in recovery.

We are told in our 12-Step program that if we are not to succumb to our old habits, our personalities must undergo change; there must be spiritual growth. And we are told that if we are to make spiritual progress, we must be willing to relinquish our will. We are told that those who have been successful in distancing themselves from their old habits have made a decision to turn their will and their lives over to a Higher Power.

Some of us have trouble dealing with any concept of a supreme being. But we are also assured that we needn't feel out of place or be discouraged, for everyone who comes to this program can at least believe that the people in our recovery group are trying to help us.

When I arrived, I was confused, frightened and defensive. But I found I could make a decision, however grudgingly, to subordinate my will to that of the group. If so many of these people had succeeded together in overcoming their compulsions, it seemed to me that a collective wisdom was at work, a concentration of experience that even someone as brilliant as I could make use of.

Later on I heard an agnostic speaker at one of our meetings say that he had to learn acceptance. "Acceptance, for instance, of the reality that some people believe in a supernatural power, and some either don't or don't know if they do. But what has saved my life is a very real *human* power called sharing."

I could buy that. I was learning to share, too. Not just criticize. And as I did share, I sensed something bigger than myself, maybe something even bigger than the group.

As I saw unexplainable changes taking place in my friends and sensed odd shifts of attitude in myself, I began to wonder. I decided we weren't quite the same people anymore and my world wasn't the same either. Eventually I found myself, along with my program friends, giving credit to a force beyond my control.

As time went on and my confidence grew, so did my dependence on this higher power, call it what we may — our Creator, our inner guide, our conscience, intuition, the power of love, the power of sharing or the personal God that we individually understand.

Old-timers in recovery helped me to see that it was to my advantage to relinquish my will to this Higher Power. My own bullheadedness could only cause me trouble, they said, and my ego was out to get me. But my Higher Power wanted me to succeed, wanted me to fulfill my destiny. I came to believe that there was a plan for this world and that somehow my life and my will were part of the plan. Naturally I wanted to know more about it, so I began the search for understanding.

All the time my well-nurtured skepticism, my caustic habit of mind was working against me. If there was a power great enough to have created this universe, which I frequently doubted, how could my puny existence play any part in it? Don't worry about it, the old-timers said. We all have doubts. It's the effort that we make to find out *what's* working in our lives that counts, they said, not *why* or *how*.

So I set out to discover, if I could, what my existence means to my Higher Power. If I tried to make friends and

learn what my Higher Power is interested in and wants
me to do, I reasoned, there's no telling what might happen
to me or what I might become. Besides . . . what did I
have to lose?

I remembered John, an ex-jailbird, talking about what
happened when he stumbled on the Third Step shortly
after he came to the program. He was a pretty tough guy
and no dummy either. He didn't know if there was a power
greater than himself, especially one he couldn't see.

"Turn my life and my will over to God as I *don't* understand him?" John asked. "What gives? How's that going to
keep me sober?"

But then John, who was five years sober when he told
me this, said he started investigating — "Out of pure
orneriness as much as anything.

"Somebody had said if I would get off my backside and
reach out a little bit and try and find out something about
this Higher Power, I'd learn something," John said. "I didn't
believe him so I decided to prove him wrong. I started
asking people about this Higher Power, what they believed
and what they did about it. And that's when some mighty
strange things started happening in my life."

In John's case, things started happening for the better.
Mine too. Things started clicking for me. And after 16
sober years in AA, I've come to the conclusion that whatever we become as a result of trying to replace our will
with our Higher Power's, there's a chance that we'll become something better than we are now.

Nevertheless getting our own will out of the way is not
simple. The 12-Step program is a simple one but it can
easily be made complicated. It takes patience and experience to get the feel of it. And it takes the help and example
of those who have gone before us. This works the same
for Al-Anon, Adult Children of Alcoholics, Overeaters
Anonymous and all the other 12-Step programs.

To hear a lot of people tell it, the Third Step is made of
rubber. We make a decision to turn our will and our lives
over to the care of God. But it bounces right back. In
Third Step discussions, we keep hearing, "I turn it over

but I always take it back."

Turning our will over is one of the great conundrums. How does one will the loss of will?

How to succeed in turning it over and leaving it with our Higher Power . . . that's the aim of this book.

- We'll find out what others have done to make it stick.
- We'll explore the mysteries of willpower and the power of relinquishing it.
- We'll discover why it is so important to our spiritual progress.
- We'll learn the value of surrender and of commitment.
- We'll talk about failure and how to break the pattern.
- We'll see what works, what doesn't and maybe find out why.
- We'll get to know our enemy as well as our best friend.
- And we'll find out what it feels like to succeed.

But first, we have to make that decision. Making the decision is the most important part and the easiest. Why not do it right now, even if you've done it before? And tell a friend you've done it.

Then we'll start working on making it stick. And we'll have plenty of help along the way. That's the way it is in this fellowship. Our friends always help and we get what we need when we need it.

1

Center Of The Universe

. . . . . .

*Our unreasonable individualism
(egocentricity if you like) was, of course,
the main reason we all failed in life
and betook ourselves
to alcohol.*

— Bill W.

In the first blush of freedom from slavery to our compulsions, many of us feel we can take on the world. Suddenly, there is nothing that we cannot do. We're apt to be full of advice for our loved ones and the people we work with. Knowing what's wrong with ourselves and, supposedly, knowing what to do about it gives us, we think, extraordinary insight into the workings of others. And some of us aren't shy about letting it be known.

But getting clean and sober, getting honest with ourselves and becoming morally responsible do not qualify us immediately to set up shop as marriage counselors, mental health experts or business tycoons — even if that's what we are. My first few months of sobriety, in fact, hardly qualified me to cross the street without a Boy Scout in tow.

Addicts have a way of going to extremes, complicating the simplest things in life, and I was no exception. My life was a jigsaw puzzle whose pieces had been mindlessly scattered, yet I expected my sobriety to bring back the missing pieces like metal filings drawn to a magnet. I expected friends and family to join in my spirit of renewal, reforming their own lives with the same enthusiasm.

In the early years of AA, some psychologists did a personality profile on several members who were enjoying newfound sobriety. These AA pioneers were found to be shockingly childish, immature and self-centered. They considered themselves to be the center of the universe — just like some people we know today, huh? Ourselves included.

Sobriety is no guarantee of mature thinking nor of a well-ordered life. While it simplified my own chaotic existence to some degree, it was hardly the magic key to successful living.

When Bill W., a co-founder of AA, had been sober for 24 years, he was by his own admission still plagued by emotional immaturity.

"Those adolescent urges that so many of us have for top approval, perfect security and perfect romance — urges quite appropriate to age 17 — prove to be an impossible way of life when we are at age 47 or 57," Bill wrote to a close friend.

"Since AA began, I've taken immense wallops in all these areas because of my failure to grow up, emotionally and spiritually."[1]

I-Centricity

I know exactly what Bill was talking about. Sixteen years into my sobriety the world is still I-centric. In any kind of disagreement, ask me if I can see the other fellow's point of view and I'll say sure. But that's not how I *feel*. I feel put upon. I feel threatened. I feel as if my good sense is being impugned and unfairly put to the test. How dare he not see things my way!

I also find myself doing things I know will get me into trouble — indulging in momentary pleasures that inevitably reward me with an emotional kick in the pants, as they have countless times before. Another favorite pastime is to chew tirelessly on a grievance that I can do nothing about. I love to nurse my wounded ego. I love to mud-wrestle with self-justification and hug resentments to my bosom.

I'm not without help, though. None of us is. The Third Step offers us a solution for what we confessed in the First Step — "That our lives had become unmanageable."

None of us is likely to be without need of this help. If the man who helped to create the granddaddy of all 12-Step programs could admit his "adolescent urges" still lingered two dozen years into sobriety, it's pretty obvious that the Third Step is for everyone. I don't have to spin out of control anymore. The Third Step offers me equilibrium.

Left to my own devices, I'm seldom capable of staying on an even keel. And I find that I'm not by myself.

Jane, a friend from Denver, beautifully illustrates my experience with her own.

"When I came into AA," she said, "I had no problem turning my drinking over to the care of God *as I understand Him*. In fact, I had already turned it over in the First Step, so what was the big deal? After all, that's what I was in AA for, to get help with my drinking. The rest of my life was mine to run. Being an intelligent, responsible, efficient, well-educated woman, there was no question I could handle any other aspect of my life."

But then, Jane said, those other aspects of her life began to unravel, one by one. "I kept finding myself in one jam after another. Each one, of course, I thought I could handle myself. It was a constant battle to make people and circumstances conform to my will. It wasn't until I had tried and failed I guess dozens of times that it began to dawn on me that something was wrong — with me."

Finally, with a nudge from her sponsor, she admitted she was powerless — "Not only over alcohol, but also over people, places and things. Not until then could I make a decision to turn *everything* over to my Higher Power. Only after I was whipped by daily living did I see the need to."

At this point something interesting happened. Jane discovered that no matter what she turned over to her Higher Power — communication with her husband, getting the kids to stop fighting, a difficult relationship at work, whatever — "The thing I turned over always improved."

Jane had a choice: Turn her will over to her Higher Power or suffer the consequences of self-will. That's the freedom of choice we all have. And we exercise it every day.

An AA lawyer from Charleston had "gone through some situations where people weren't doing quite what I wanted them to."

Poor Vincent. Witnesses weren't showing up for depositions, court clerks were forgetting appointments and misplacing files, judges were immune to logic. He found himself in a scheduling nightmare and it was driving him nuts.

"They really upset my apple cart," Vincent said. "And I could see the paranoia and the negative thinking setting back in. I suffered from it . . . even though I recognized it for what it was, it was no use."

Poor Vincent. His self-pity ballooned to monstrous proportions and he felt helpless to do anything about it. What had happened suddenly to his long-cultivated serenity? Why, after 15 years of sobriety and faithful attendance at countless meetings, was everything going wrong?

"Suddenly one day I prayed. I prayed for those people who were causing me trouble. I prayed for that situation. I just kept praying. And gradually, little by little, it occurred to me that *I* might be at fault. It occurred to me that I'm still a sick alcoholic."

Soul sickness, or a dry drunk as it's commonly known, is no respecter of age or experience. It plays no favorites. Although Vincent has one of these painful lapses every now and then, they don't go on for too long before he tumbles to what ails him.

One Day At A Time

"We're told in this program that we can never cure our alcoholism or other addiction, that all we can do is arrest it on a daily basis," he said. "And arresting that disease is contingent upon our spiritual condition.

"My disease is not alcohol," Vincent says. "Alcohol diagnosed my disease. My disease is my underlying self-centeredness."

I can't argue with him. It's mine too. But that doesn't mean I'm a hopeless case any more than Vincent is. Millions of recovering people who are living happy productive lives can attest to making progress against self-centeredness, giving credit where it is due — to practicing the 12 Steps. Many of those people no doubt would say that their success in overcoming life's frustrations is due to varying degrees of willingness to turn their will and their lives over to the care of a Higher Power.

For self-centered people, that may be a tough job. But it needn't be tackled all at once. Willingness usually is enough to get one started and unlike most jobs, we've all got the qualifications — no experience necessary. But acknowledging the existence of something larger than our own towering ego does seem to be asking a lot.

We're not saints. How can ordinary people do the impossible? It's like addiction. We turn it loose, glance around and — look out! — here it is right back in our laps.

Trying just to do what our Higher Power wants us to do — relinquish our will — shouldn't be as hard as this but it is, isn't it? Ask anybody. It's about as easy as qualifying for sainthood and we're not up to that. We're not even interested in that.

At this point we're about ready to give up the whole idea. But something's tugging at our shirtsleeves. A tiny voice asks, "What if?"

What if it were really possible?

2

A Pattern Of Failure

. . . . . .

*One of the reasons mature
people stop learning is that they become less
and less willing to risk failure.*

— John W. Gardner

e've all been through it. The resolve to do better. To stop doing this, to begin doing that. We've got to quit smoking. Watch our cholesterol. Start exercising. Be more thoughtful. Count our calories. Watch our tempers. Take time to smell the roses. Show our appreciation. Say our prayers. Read a good book. Quit biting our nails. Eat less ice cream. Take our vitamins. Get more sleep. Watch less television. And so on.

The reason New Year's resolutions get so much attention is that hope soars skyward but promises crash like a windless kite. It's human nature to reach high and fall short. And to believe it'll be different next time.

So it always was with our self-destructive behaviors. We always thought it would be different the next time we indulged. We would be in control next time. Nothing would go wrong because we would watch it, we would be more careful. And of course it never worked. Like the kite, we always crashed.

Consequently for those of us in 12-Step programs, the idea of attempting something noble — even something humbling — is disheartening. The thought of failure is ever with us.

Until I hit bottom and asked for help in AA, I was not able to stop drinking. I had promised myself thousands of times but promises are quickly forgotten in the throes of withdrawal. Because of my repeated fruitless attempts to stop killing myself, you might say I was programmed for failure.

I am so accustomed to trying and failing that it is second nature to me now. I failed to control my behavior so often that I lost my self-respect. Because I was a victim of disease, not weak will, I can now see that this was inevitable. The results of trying to gain control were foregone conclusions. Everyone who knew me could have predicted the ending. Everyone but me. Yet deep inside I knew too that with each attempt I would fail once again.

This was a common trait with most of us. That's why we try to live one day at a time. When we set our sights on a goal today, suddenly we're likely to experience that old gut-clutching panic. We weren't very good at carrying out resolutions then, and we're probably not a whole lot better at it now. So we're apt to be careful about making promises to ourselves or anyone else. We don't want to go through another humiliating failure.

It's a common fear. So it's only natural to balk at trying something as strange and as seemingly impossible as turning our will over to a Higher Power. Look at our track record. We can make pledges, we can promise but what's always happened when we've done that? Failure.

There's one difference about our good intentions with the Third Step, though. We don't have to promise ourselves anything. We aren't making a resolution here. There are no promises to break. No self-esteem to drag in the dirt. No fears to resurrect. We are only asked to make a decision.

A decision is neither promise nor pledge. It is just something we make up our mind to do. There is no time limit on a decision, nor is there a penalty if we fail.

Daily Decision

If we make the decision to turn our will and our life over to our Higher Power today and find ourselves back in the driver's seat tomorrow, what have we lost? Nothing. Instead we have gained. We have been in touch with our Higher Power, no harm in that. If we have made the decision to turn our will over to our Higher Power today, we are one up on yesterday. Why not ignore tomorrow?

Besides, if every day we turn our will over to our Higher Power and then take it back . . . well, we have simply become people who make contact every day with our Higher Power. There's something to be said for that.

"What are you worrying about?" asked an old-timer. "Babe Ruth struck out 1,330 times."

Our sponsors tell us over and over that if we're having trouble with a Step maybe we should return to the one before it.

"All I needed to take Step 3 was to accept the help that was offered in Step 2," said one sponsor. To me that meant making a decision to turn my will over would be a little easier when I reminded myself that I could get help from *"a Power greater than ourselves."*

In many cases, it's a good idea to go all the way back to Step 1, *admitting all over again that we are powerless.* Sometimes, it's essential.

If we are to be successful with Step 3, another old-timer said, "We have to experience Step 1 a hundred percent — surrender, accept and become willing." I took it he meant that making a decision is almost impossible unless I've surrendered to and accepted the fact that my old way just didn't work.

Katie, a tough little Irish actress, said Step 1 was the only way she could come to terms with Step 3.

"The First Step to me is my life," she explained. "The rest of it is gravy. The first step's the turkey, and without it there ain't no Thanksgiving. The longer I'm in, the more I realize the more and more things I'm powerless over.

And the strange thing is, just like with the drinking and drugging, once I accept that I'm powerless over a situation, when I've surrendered to that, I get everything I need."

Katie said it was hard for her to understand that somehow when she gave up, she was stronger. And she had trouble acknowledging the "higher" in Higher Power.

"I had been my own higher power for so many years. I was the controller in every relationship I had. So how could I release control over my will to a disembodied higher power?"

The answer came to her, she said, from the Big Book (Alcoholics Anonymous), which says alcoholics have to "quit playing God." Instead, it says, we have to depend on God. We have to trust Him.

In Step 1, Katie said, "I had to do more than admit, I had to accept. In Step 3, I had to do more than believe, I had to trust. For me, this Step was the beginning of trust."

Trusting is to believing what accepting is to admitting. It puts us a little closer in touch.

Charlie, a veteran who has been retired longer than some of us have been alive, told this story at an AA convention:

"I had been in the program just a few weeks when I became aware of the potential power of Step 3. People talked about it in meetings and my sponsor lived it. Aha! I thought, so this is the secret!"

The night it dawned on him that Step 3 was the key to great power, he couldn't wait to get home and get on his knees. "Take over, God," he prayed, and slept like a baby. But the next morning, he said, "I took it all back again without even knowing it. By nightfall I realized what I had done, and I turned it over again. So it went, back and forth, back and forth."

He didn't know he was practicing. But that's what it was. He practiced turning it over until he got good at it or at least better.

"After nearly 40 years, though, I'm still practicing. You know, even old-timers need practice."

Maybe we ought to take another look at what we've
been asked to do — simply to decide to turn our will and
our lives over to the care of the power that broke our
pattern of repeated failure and restored our self-respect.
For that, we can at least *make a decision to become willing to
make a decision* once every day.

3

Fear Of The Unknown

. . . . . .

And I will show you something different from either
Your shadow at morning striding behind you,
Or your shadow at evening rising to meet you.
I will show you fear in a handful of dust.

— T.S. Eliot

T o give up our will — think about it — that's asking an awful lot. It's an unnatural act. I had been trained since childhood to exert my will. Most of us have. It's the means by which we accomplish our goals, mold our characters, make something of ourselves. And now . . . just give it up? Try to pretend it is no longer ours? That's a tall order.

This was to be no ordinary experiment either. I was being asked to turn my will — my whole life, in fact — over to the care of some force that I could neither see nor hear. A benign force, I was assured, but nonetheless one completely unknown to me, except for the stern unresponsive father figure to whom I prayed as a child. What was the difference now? Wasn't this still the same unknowable, uncommunicative God that would not answer my questions or calm my misgivings?

Was I skeptical? Of course. Was I afraid? Of course. Because this was supposed to have something to do with whether I stayed sober or not.

It's a fear shared by a lot of newcomers. We are afraid because we don't know what's going to happen if we go through with it — if we *can* go through with it. We are afraid of the unknown. We are afraid of change.

Don't talk to Beth about change. She is a nurse who "stayed in some absolutely terrible situations that I loathed and despised," she said at an AA meeting.

"Yet rather than step over and take a chance on some things that I had no experience with, I stayed where I was. I refused to make a move," Beth said.

"If anybody asked, 'How are you?' my answer was always, 'Fine,'" she said. "Because I knew if I said I wasn't fine, the next question would be, 'Well, what are you doing about it?' and my answer would have to be, 'Not a damned thing.'

"I carried that same habit pattern right into sobriety," Beth said. "For three years I wouldn't make a move until, finally coming to my knees, I found there truly was a power greater than myself."

The Hardest Lesson

Angie, a housewife, said she knew what Beth meant. When it was suggested to Angie that she turn her will over, she froze.

"I could handle 'One day at a time,' and, you know, 'Don't pick up a drink,' but the rest of it really sucked," she said. "At least that's what I thought at the time. Yet eventually I learned I had to give up." Even so, it was one of the hardest things she had to do, she said.

"I have always been so dreadfully afraid that I wasn't going to get what I wanted and the fear of simply standing alone and relying on God was frightening."

Fred, a carpenter who plays the horses on the side, said he didn't know much about turning his will over, but he understood the fear of change.

"I'm at Aqueduct Race Track in New York with a $250 suit on and no money to get back to New Jersey," Fred said. "But that's normal. Not playing the horses — that's *not* normal. That's change and it makes me nervous."

Mike is willing to be nervous. A 24-year-old lifeguard with three years of sobriety, he said he "didn't come to this program to be unhappy, and if it takes changing what

I'm doing to get me out of being unhappy, I'm going to have a go at it, nervous or not.

"Besides," he said, "turning my will over kind of appeals to me because making my own decisions usually ends up making me unhappy. And that's very important for me to know because I've been told over and over again that if I'm not happy, I will pick up a drink. Then sooner or later, I'll get drunk."

Desperation made some of us more willing to change than others. Beachcomber John is a case in point. He had gone all the way to the bottom. He was a derelict and believed in nothing but survival. Because the will to survive was strong enough, when he got to AA, he said he was willing to change, even though he didn't believe in God.

"I think I was *willing* to believe in God, though, and I realized that my will was not conforming to any kind of God I had heard about," John said. "So any change they wanted me to make was going to be all right with me."

Painful Change

Change is inevitable and, unfortunately, painful. It means the old, the familiar and the comfortable are being replaced. When we enter new and strange surroundings, we feel discombobulated. We feel psychic pain. Pain, though, is something we neither can nor should try to avoid. It is a reality of life, a normal human experience and an efficient teacher.

When we take the wrong things into our bodies or minds, they sound the alarm, sending out signals of pain. Confusion and dreadful bouts of mental and physical debilitation are other signals that alcoholics and dope addicts are well aware of. The irony is that in attempting to escape pain, addicts create even more agony for themselves and those who love them.

So change is not comfortable. It can be painful. And useful.

Straitjacket Jerry has seen a lot of change in his life, and a lot of pain. "Like many others, I decided I had my life well in hand. It didn't matter that I had drunk myself right out of a good business and my partner had deserted me. I wasn't insane just because I had gone back to drinking after I nearly died, after they had me in the looney bin in a straitjacket, being on a resuscitator, losing my pulse, being given up for lost and all the rest."

"Throughout it all," Jerry said, "I believed in a Higher Power. Maybe because I was still alive.

"But when it came to turning my will over, I couldn't do it," he said. "I was in pretty bad shape when I first came in, but I still wasn't in bad enough shape to swallow the whole program. I didn't want to lose control."

Losing Control

Aha. Another fear surfaces — fear of losing control, just one more aspect of the unknown. What happens when we lose control? We know some of the things that used to happen when we lost control and can only guess at some of the other things that happened. But what about now?

Wait a minute. Wait just a blooming minute. What is this about losing control?

Does anyone here *have* control? Yes? Then they must be in the wrong program.

After all, haven't we already admitted that we were powerless? Hadn't we always failed until we came to this program, conceding defeat and asking for help? We surrendered, remember? And what was it we surrendered? The idea that we could control our compulsions, of course. That was the First Step. So what's so different about giving up control now? Control of our will and our lives. What's different about turning our will and our lives over to God as suggested in the Third Step? It's just another act of surrender.

One difference may be that we're conscious of it now. We know what we're being asked to do. When we came to this program, we weren't aware of much of anything beyond the need to get help. We were beaten and were willing to accept any answer that worked. And now that it is working we begin to question it. We begin rationalizing.

And the ego's arguments are insistent: Do I really want to turn my will over? After all, I am ultimately responsible for whatever I do. They can talk all they want about how this is a disease but I'm in possession of my senses *now*. I'm in control. I can't just lightly give it up. What if my Higher Power made me tell my boss what I think of him? What if I lost my job and my wife left me? Hey, this is serious business.

Sure it is. And it's perfectly natural after being in the program a little while or a long while, to feel as if we're in charge of our actions. Our life is starting to straighten out. There's some semblance of order now. We're not so confused and frightened. Neither are those around us. So it's only natural for us to think that we have something to do with it and we don't want to give that up.

"When things start going good," said Laura in a First Step discussion, "then I start thinking I'm in control or that I'm getting a handle on my life or a particular situation. And then it seems as if something always comes along and brings me down to the right size, to show me again that I'm powerless."

Sure, when things are going well we tend to think it's because we have been conducting our lives with consummate skill. In fact, though, we could make no progress at all (remember?) until we admitted that we were powerless and that our lives were unmanageable. Beyond asking for help, we have nothing to do with our recovery. Our Higher Power, on the other hand, has everything to do with it.

Fear of change, fear of the unknown, fear of losing control are all legitimate concerns. But we have to look at the guiding force behind all the advice we've been getting.

That guiding force is unconditional love and by any other name that's God, as I understand God. Unconditional love seeks only our good. It cannot want anything else for us. Therefore, it can be trusted.

4

Getting Your
Feet Wet

· · · · · ·

*The profundity of a spiritual act
is in direct proportion to its
author's commitment.*

— Henri De Lubac

E veryone who learns to swim has to get into the water. This is always frightening to beginners, whether standing on the bank of a river, teetering on the edge of a swimming pool or dipping a toe in the ocean's brine. Yet at some point, if we are to learn whether the water will welcome us, we have to put aside our fears and jump in.

It's called commitment.

When I was two years old, I waded into a lake over my head. My mother pulled me out. I didn't know any better. It was the only way I knew to find out what would happen. Later when I was five, I stepped off of a pier into a river. That was unintentional, and once again my mother fished me out. In both cases I learned something about water. I also learned something about dependence. I found out I could rely on my mother to keep me from drowning.

Making a Third Step commitment is the only way to find out what will happen when we turn our wills and our lives over to something that's not under our control. It's just as scary as jumping off a pier, especially if we've never been in that particular river. So our tendency is to just stick with the toe-dipping. We don't want to get carried away with this thing, do we?

For instance, we may be kind of toying with the intriguing idea of discovering our inner world. We are told it's a place of quiet stillness, and we could sure use some of that. We are told that within our very being we can find peace — no confusion and strife, no noise or turmoil. And we are told we don't have to look for it in church or even call it religion. Instead, if we want, we can call it therapy or mental health.

But then we hear in our 12-Step program that at some point we'll need to make a commitment, and this is a rude sort of shock.

"It is easy to forget God when one is most concerned about one's inner experiences," says Gregory Vlastos in *The Religious Way*. "It is not so easy to forget Him when one is concerned about commitment . . .. To talk about commitment brings one face to face with the question of God, so that one cannot dodge it."

Vlastos insists that people must eventually make a choice about the direction they will take.

The Choice To Love

"We have tried the ways of ambition, of self-aggrandizement, of aggressive opportunism and we have seen the kind of flimsy success to which they lead. We have tasted the bitter poisons they generate, we have known the conflict, the disgust, the inner division, the outer isolation that follow in their wake. We have also tried in some small measure the other way, and known that every man and woman must have love, that there is no life or peace without love, only strife, waste, madness, destruction, death."

That pretty well characterizes my life under the influence of addiction. When mired in self-centeredness and self-destruction, my life was chaos. I lacked love. Under the influence of alcohol and other mind-altering drugs, I lacked the ability to express it or feel it — the one key ingredient that could restore me to meaningful living. Love brought me out of the pit of despair. It brought all of us together in our 12-Step programs, helping one another by loving one another. What else is there to choose?

"There is that in life which makes it necessary that men should find the way of truth," Vlastos says.

"You cannot live a day or an hour without saying either yes or no to it . . .. The alternatives are simple — terrifyingly simple and clear. To compromise in this matter is to decide; to waver is to decide; to postpone and evade decision is to decide; to hide the matter is to decide. There is no escape. You must say yes or no. There are a thousand ways of saying no; one way of saying yes and no way of saying anything else."[1]

Still, many of us are not sure at first. Most people in 12-Step programs are in one way or another coerced into joining. Pain, despair, humiliation, family pressure, job pressure, whatever — we are being nudged, shoved and kicked in the rear end when we come to this program. And we may feel still more negative pressure as we come to face the Third Step.

If we've been going it alone, ignoring the help of a power greater than ourselves, we may be feeling a lot of uncertainty. Chances are we're pretty unhappy. Chances are that our misery is pushing us to the brink of commitment.

The Rev. Edward J. Dowling, S.J., a Roman Catholic priest who helped Bill W. with the Fifth Step, talked about the alcoholic's "negative road to salvation."

"The negative road is perfectly fine," he said at an AA conference. "Why, sometimes I think that if I *ever* get to heaven, it will be from backing away from hell."

That's okay. It doesn't matter how or why we take the plunge, just so we do it.

If we're typical, after jumping in, we'll be elated. Just diving off that river bank, once and for all, takes a load off our minds. Even though we are well aware of our long history of failing to live up to promises of self-improvement, we are likely to find ourselves suddenly feeling very enthusiastic.

After a time, of course, we discover that we are lounging on shore again, high and dry, without even realizing that we had pulled ourselves back to terra firma. It's not unexpected. In fact, it's almost certain to happen. But that's okay. It's only natural to start out on a new venture with enthusiasm and then back off, retreating to the familiar and comfortable.

Feeling a little guilty, we get back in the swim, then relapse again. The old familiar pattern has reasserted itself. With each repetition of commitment-failure-recommitment, our guilt grows. Finally as frustration increases, we give up.

"I just can't make it stick," we say. "I'm too used to running the show. This is not for me."

But having felt faith's invigorating splash in the face, the comfortable buoyancy of trust in a Higher Power even momentarily, we can never again be satisfied with living on the river bank, where we are dry, lonely and scared.

The Leap Of Faith

Commitment to the Third Step is a leap in the dark, a journey into the unknown. We can try to prepare for it, but there is just no way of knowing in advance what will happen to us. It's like getting married. No matter how long we've known our partner or how well we think we know each other's traits or how committed we think we are, there's no substitute for tying the knot. Something changes at that point. When we have experienced it, we are not quite the same person we were before.

Once we have experienced the leap of faith, we are irrevocably changed. Even if we revoke our commitment, never again will we be able to wonder what it is like to trust another being, even momentarily. After commitment, we know what it is like. We were there. It's something like having traveled to a foreign land. Never again will we wonder what that country is like. We were there.

We are no longer strangers to the sights and sounds of that once unfamiliar place. Being there changes our perspective. Whether we stay or return to our homeland, the change is forever.

It is clear, though, that we do not change ourselves. Instead, we are changed. That's what's so mysterious and exciting about the Third Step. There's little we have to do. It is done to us and for us. The reason that we are almost certain to pick ourselves up and dive back in again is not that we have got faith but that it has got us.

Still, we can help it along. There are things we can do to interrupt the commitment-failure-recommitment cycle. Bill W. talks about the proper use of willpower in the book *Twelve Steps and Twelve Traditions*, pointing out, "There are certain things which only the individual can do. All by himself, and in the light of his own circumstances, he needs to develop the quality of willingness. When he acquires willingness, he is the only one who can make the decision to exert himself. Trying to do this is an act of his own will. All of the 12-Steps require sustained and personal exertion to conform to their principles and so, we trust, to God's will."

He is quick to emphasize that last point: "It is when we try to make our will conform with God's that we begin to use it rightly.

"To all of us this was a most wonderful revelation. Our whole trouble had been the misuse of willpower. We had tried to bombard our problems with it instead of attempting to bring it into agreement with God's intention for us."[2]

It can be assumed that one of God's intentions for us is to trust God. So anything we can do to bring that about through the exertion of willpower has got to be okay.

It's not easy for some of us to put our trust in a Higher Power. But if we are willing to put some trust in our fellow humans, especially those whose lives have been transformed in this program, we have made a beginning. When we practice trusting someone other than ourselves, we are on our way to commitment. Of course, those of us

who use the group as our Higher Power have no problem
with that anyway. We already do trust human beings. We
gave them a certain amount of trust when we first asked
for help, and that trust inevitably has grown.

A strange thing happens when we trust our companions. They become worthy of it. They were, of course,
deserving of our trust all along, but now we can see it
where we couldn't before. Practicing trust of humans usually increases our ability to trust a Higher Power.

A Hindu proverb goes like this: "Help thy brother's boat
across and lo! Thine own has reached the shore." A good
way to increase our own faith is to help our brothers and
sisters realize theirs. We learn by teaching.

Practice, Practice, Practice

Most of all, we learn to trust by practicing. "Through
the help of human beings in these rooms," says Merle, a
New Hampshire social worker, "I have watched in amaze-
ment as my fears and worries slowly dissipated. It happened as I began to feel that the strangers I met here
might really care what happened to me. Soon I knew they
did. Wanting to care and feel as they did has kept me
coming back, and it has kept me working at a relationship
with my Higher Power.

"But it hasn't been easy," Merle says. "Obtaining some
semblance of faith in a power greater than me has been a
constant struggle. The patterns of failure deeply em-
bedded in my mind keep emerging, and I keep trying to
replace them with rational thinking.

"Finally, I realized what others had been saying all along.
They said that if I was to have faith, I had to practice it.
It was a profound realization. Many times I had turned
my will and life over to the care of God as I understood
Him, but I wasn't praying as I heard others say they did on
a daily, sometimes hourly basis. If I wanted faith, I had to
act like it. I had to be in touch with my Higher Power all
the time."

In order to have faith we must practice it. When we do, our commitment grows stronger. Commitment is the blending of faith into daily living. It makes possible an automatic turning to our Higher Power whenever we feel any uncertainty about what we are doing or what direction we should take, even in the smallest, most insignificant things. Nothing is insignificant to our Higher Power. Everything contributes to what we are and what we will become.

Once committed, we don't have to strain for faith. There's no need to.

B.B., a San Francisco AA, writing in the *Grapevine*, told of a white-knuckle ride on a roller coaster, where he was tensing at every dip and turn. It was grim business.

"I shut my eyes, ducked my head, and held on. . .. When we arrived safely at the other end, I was still holding on. As I walked out of the exit, I had more trouble steering a straight line than I did during my last drunk." B.B. said he tried to figure out why that ride was so upsetting to his serenity, and he remembered that some of the passengers had held their hands over their heads instead of gripping the safety bar.

"At the time I thought they were suicidal," B.B. said. "But then I realized what they were doing . . . surrendering."

The next time he rode the roller coaster, he tried relaxing instead of fighting it every inch of the way.

"I found that if I sat back and let the car carry me where it wanted to go, I didn't have to fight. The secret was to relax and enjoy it. All I needed was blind faith that I could somehow get through the ride unscathed, that the whole structure wasn't going to collapse under me. All I had to do was pay for the ticket and then ride. It was my ticket but I wasn't in the driver's seat. In other words, I had to let go and turn it over."

A friend wanted to know if this was one of B.B.'s "complicated allegories, where the roller coaster represents your Higher Power and the car is AA, and . . .."

"No," said B.B. "I was only talking about how to ride a roller coaster. Now be quiet. The meeting is about to start."[3]

Shhh. Don't mention this to B.B., but if we choose to apply his non-allegory to working our own Third Step, he probably won't sue us.

5

The
Chief Clown

· · · · · ·

*There's only one thing that
can keep growing without nourishment:
the human ego.*

— Marshall Lumsden

I f we are to have any success at letting go and turning it over, we'll have to climb out of our emotional roller coaster and face the operator. Our stomach-churning ups and downs are all orchestrated by an arrogant little prankster known as our ego. This is the conductor of our train, the captain of our ship, the chief clown of our circus. This is the creator of all our discontent, the author of all our confusion, the instigator of all our anger.

We tend to think that our anger stems from the selfish, heedless and irrational attitudes and actions of other people or from the lousy cards that fate has dealt us. Our anger, we think, is appropriate and entirely justified. Anger always seems to be a logical response to whatever disagreeable thing is happening to us. But it is really not caused by anything or anyone outside ourselves.

For me, anger is a choice, instantaneous and fleeting though the decision may be. It is the product of my own inflated ego. In every instance, it is my *will* to be angry. It's a decision that comes from within. Anger can flare up so quickly that I may be able to catch only a glimpse of that decision-making process. If I'm doing a slow burn, it's easier to spot. Most times I can't see it at all. But in every instance it has something to do with my pride or

my sense of what's right and wrong. I've watched myself
getting angry often enough to know that it is a choice.

If we are to make progress in turning over our will to
a higher authority, we have to recognize that for every
action we take to relinquish it, there will be a roughly
equal reaction from our ego to hang onto it.

This doesn't mean we can't succeed. But we must get
used to the idea that the turning loose of our will is not a
popular notion in every corner of our psyche. Our ego
thinks we are nuts to suggest such a thing. We may be
sure that it will have something to say about it over and
over again.

Our ego, of course, has something to say about every
thought we have. It is the self-appointed judge of all we
think and do. It is also the self-appointed judge of everyone we come into contact with. The ego looks upon no
one impartially.

An Exercise On Thinking

Let's try a little experiment. Find a quiet place where
you won't be interrupted and spend an hour or so recording your thoughts, either with a notebook or a tape re-
corder. Get into a comfortable position and make sure
that for the next hour you won't be distracted. Unplug
the telephone, muffle the doorbell, turn off the radio or
TV and do whatever else is necessary to be able to pay
attention to your thoughts and nothing else.

Do not actually focus on your thinking, but just let
your mind wander until you suddenly realize that it has
picked out some person or situation for attention. As soon
as you recognize what it is your mind is doing, record it.
Jot down a notation about everything your mind alights
on. A very brief description of your thoughts will do, just
enough for you to recall it later. Who or what you are
thinking about is not as important as your attitude toward
that person or situation. Be sure to record your feelings

and your assessments. What about them? What are the people doing right or wrong? How does it affect you?

To be absolutely fair, you should quit reading now and not pick up this book again until you have tried the experiment at the first opportunity. If you keep reading now, it is liable to color your perception of what happens during your period of mental observation. Knowing that you are watching for a certain thing, your ego may try to keep you from catching it in the act.

Not that it matters too much. Being warned about what's going to happen isn't likely to change the contents of your mental meanderings for long. Your ego cannot put off its favorite activity forever. In all probability, it will focus on what is nearest and dearest to it — anything that reinforces its sense of imperial majesty — regardless of whether you are watching or not. It is chiefly concerned with proving to its own satisfaction — and yours — that everyone else is, well . . . you'll see.

Don't let your mind stay on one subject. As soon as you have put down some thoughts about one thing, instruct it to move on. Your ego likes to dwell on a subject until it exhausts all possibilities, then starts repeating itself. Don't let it.

Once the hour is up, if you have carefully recorded each episode of thought, what you are holding in your hand is an indictment of everyone who came to mind. This may not hold true if you have just fallen in love or if you are in a particularly happy frame of mind when you try the experiment. But in almost every other context, your ego will be having a field day with all the people it considers inferior to it. And that's everyone. For your ego has never met a person it didn't find fault with.

Its ability to criticize, demean, scorn and ridicule is legendary. It wallows in grievances. No matter who it is or how much you may love the person, the ego has other ideas. It goes straight for the jugular.

During the time you let your mind drift, you probably noticed that it was nurturing grievances against almost everyone who crossed your mind. It was engaged in defending itself while picking this one and that one apart, finding fault, keeping score, building a case. These are ego habits. *It's what the ego does for a living.*

No one is saintly enough to measure up to the ego's standards. Nothing ever turns out the way the ego thinks it should. It is a merciless critic, a carping complainer, a never-satisfied grouch.

It isn't possible, in fact, to cast our thoughts forward or backward in time without immediately beginning to assemble evidence of guilt. If our thoughts are not firmly anchored in the present, then our ego has them out scouting for someone to pin the blame on. Our ego is prosecutor, judge and jury. Any remembrance of past events, any rehashing of happenings that are finished is circumstantial evidence of guilt. Any anticipation of the future, any anxiety about what is yet to come is ready to be played out in the ego's courtroom.

Addicted To Anger

K.P., an alcoholic from Seattle, said that during her first few years of sobriety she never let on that she, like many of us, was filled with anger.

"Like many a drunk before me, I began to nip on the sly — not drinks at first, but just little sips of anger," she said. "I practiced this controlled resentment in the private closet of my own mind, usually when I retired for the night. Then as I tossed and turned, trying to sleep, the world became a courtroom. I stood pitted against those I felt had aggrieved me.

"Every night some new person — my boss, my mother, my sister, my friend — had trespassed against me," K.P. said. "Sometimes I had trespassed against them and they had the audacity to tell me about it. So off to the dream trial we went. When I awoke each morning, the resentment smoldered stronger and brighter than before."

Eventually, K.P. said, she started drinking again — after eight years of sobriety.

There's a saying in AA: "First you go crazy, then you drink again." In K.P.'s case, first she got angry. And kept nurturing it. Her ego's favorite occupation made her crazy.

Five months later, K.P.'s friends in the program welcomed her back, but her anger hadn't vanished. Her ego, bruised but undaunted, was lying in wait.

"About nine months into my new recovery, the nightly courtroom scenes began again," she said. "As the list of those aggrieving me began to grow, I knew that I was in trouble and that my old ways would no longer suffice."

She turned to the Big Book. She began to review her day as she went to bed each night and asked God to show her how to learn from it.

"But part of me still rebelled. Hadn't my husband left me when I really needed him? Wasn't my boss a shrew by anyone's standards? Weren't my creditors selfish to want to collect from a poor drunk who had been as sick as I was? I started to laugh. The 'evidence' I had so carefully garnered to prove once again that I was right stood clearly before me.

"I returned to the dreaded bed where my personal courtroom usually raged. I allowed each person against whom I bore grudges to appear. Then rather than pursue the fantasy arguments in which we all ended as losers, I simply envisioned sending each of them love from my heart, just as AAs do for me as I sit flawed before them."

K.P. found an alternative to the ego's way of handling things. She no longer performs nightly in her inner courtroom. She has given it to her Higher Power. Instead of playing judge and jury, she practices gratitude, finding that her defects are being "lifted from me in ways I could never have imagined on my own."[1]

K.P.'s mental courtroom battles are familiar to most of us. As long as anger and resentment control our thoughts, we are as vulnerable to our compulsions as we ever were. Either we turn our anger over to our Higher Power or we embrace unhappiness and danger. Yet our ego is willing to fight to the death for the right to be unhappy. It would rather preside over our destruction than lose any control.

The ego, of course, considers itself our protector. When we blame it for keeping us upset, it protests that it is only guarding us from our enemies and that everything it conjures up is for our own good. It has only our best interests at heart. With a protector like this, who needs enemies?

6

The Jack-In-The-Box
Connection

· · · · · ·

*The burden of the absolute ego is
the chief agony of life.*

— Waldo Frank

I f we are to turn our will and our lives over to the care of our Higher Power, then we must do something about the ego. Without help, dealing with the ego is a painful process. But the one to whom we are trying to surrender will provide the means for combating this nemesis, this common enemy.

When we ask our Higher Power for help in overcoming the urgings of our ego, we get the help we need. Just as we make a decision to turn our will and lives over to the care of God as we understand Him, so can we make a decision to overcome that great array of self-made beliefs that we call the ego.

Since I think of my ego as an accumulation of all the things I've learned, beginning in childhood, I don't consider its judgment to be too reliable. It's loaded with contradictions. For instance, a jack-in-the-box is supposed to be fun but my first exposure to one startled and scared me. I quickly learned what a harmless entertaining toy it was, but my ego hasn't forgotten its first encounter with the jack-in-the-box.

At the age of three, I was spanked for calling out "Fatty!" to a woman walking in front of our house. I also still carry the vestiges of shame for the punishment I received for wetting my pants at inappropriate times. Conflicting lessons I learned as an adolescent about sex are still with me despite an education that contributed to an otherwise healthy attitude toward sex.

All of our painful childhood learning experiences are stored inside and our ego uses them indiscriminately to make its judgments. Is it any wonder that we often feel confused and angry when we let the ego make decisions for us?

"The Holy Spirit, like the ego, is a decision," says *A Course In Miracles*. "Together they constitute all the alternatives the mind can accept and obey. The Holy Spirit and the ego are the only choices open to you. God created one, and so you cannot eradicate it. You made the other, and so you can. Only what God creates is irreversible and unchangeable."[1]

Because the ego is of our own making, regardless of how innocently much of it was constructed, we can change it. With enough time and faith, we might even get rid of it. We can certainly subdue it.

Although the ego is full of contradictions and its fears largely imaginary, it nevertheless has tremendous power over us. It will continue to have power as long as we respect it as our adviser. That's hard not to do. Everything the ego believes, we taught it. For most of our lives we have lived in fear, which is why it counsels fear. For most of our lives we have been angry that people seldom did what we wanted them to, which is why its response to most people and situations is anger. It is only teaching us what we taught it.

That's why now we must teach it differently. Our ego talks to us all the time. Why shouldn't we talk back?

Ego Control

First, we might try telling it that its function is to serve us, not the other way around, and repeat it often. Try this: "I need support — not fear, not anger, not confusion. If you don't have anything good to say, don't say anything."

Each time we notice our ego beating up on someone, we need to reason with it.

We might say, "That's a fellow human being you're talking about. We're all in this together, you know, so lay off. That person is our equal in every way and just as much in need of love and understanding as we are. If you don't have anything good to say about someone then don't say anything."

There's nothing wrong with a little repetition. After all, that's how we originally taught our ego, and that's the way our ego has gained its power over us: relentless repetition.

An ego that is properly nourished with selflessness, humility, helpfulness and love has got a chance to blossom into a halfway decent adviser. As long as we have to listen to it, we might as well make sure that what it has to say is worth listening to.

When it begins to catch on, when it starts feeding us thoughts of love instead of anger, we can reward it appropriately.

But first there are some things it has to learn.

One is that we are not victims. "I am not the victim of the world I see"[2] is the title of a daily lesson in *A Course in Miracles* that bears repeating over and over.

"Something that helps me," says an addict from Hutchinson, Kansas, "is trying to give up the notion that I am a victim of circumstances. Everything I've been through, and everything that I'll experience in the future, I think is a necessary part of my life and something I can learn from. I'm not a victim, I'm a learner."

This is not an easy idea to swallow, especially for those of us who have grown up under the influence of alcoholic parents or who have seen other loved ones betray, humiliate and brutalize us. But I have to remember two things. One, forgiveness is possible, no, necessary. Two, when my ego pushes the panic button, it is reacting to a history of fearful bondage, not the reality of peaceful freedom.

The ego has to learn that the past is over and done with. It cannot be changed.

There Is Only Now

Another thing our ego has to learn is that the past is over and done with. It cannot be changed. Change takes place, if at all, only here and now. Yet the ego seeks constantly to change the past. It relives our history over and over again, rewording conversations, making new choices, escaping embarrassment, punishing evildoers, correcting mistakes, tidying up all the loose ends. The ego must be taught that this is a futile occupation. It consumes exorbitant amounts of time, brainpower and emotion — all to no avail. We must remind it of that constantly.

Next, it must be taught that the future cannot yet be experienced. The ego is constantly writing scripts and issuing casting calls for the next play. It is a tireless director who takes great satisfaction in running our character and the other players through their paces, telling them what to do, how to look and what to say, warning them of dangers to avoid. We must instruct it that all this rehearsing is of no use because nothing actually happens until *now* and seldom does it happen according to script.

Then our ego needs to see that it is only fooling itself when it tries to wipe out past guilt and protect us from future harm. As it argues away our guilt, it is selecting particular scenes for evidence and ignoring others. It does the same in trying to demystify the future. It selects what it wants to happen, ignoring what is just as likely to occur.

Finally our ego must be taught that its habitual activities of reliving the past and trying to experience the future before it arrives do not make us safe and secure, do not make us happy. We can only be happy *now*.

The more often we remind ourselves of these things, the less powerful our egos become.

The single most effective thing we can do, though, is to distance ourselves from these preoccupations of the mind. Regardless of what the ego thinks, it is not in charge. *We* are. It is not up to the ego to decide what will occupy our minds. That is *our* province. The ego may be the prosecutor but it is not the judge. We are fully capable of assuming the role of judge — of which thoughts to entertain and which to show the door. In fact, we *must* if we are to have peace.

When confronted with a grievance that the ego has dredged up, we have a choice. We can obsessively wallow in resentment, as we often do. We can temporarily put it out of our minds. Or we can permanently banish it from our consciousness.

Banishing it is not a simple thing to do. The ego is much too stubborn and crafty to let us deprive it forever of one of its favorite pastimes.

We can, however, and with some ease, step away from a grievance. Whenever one appears, we can deliberately choose to think of something else. The greatest potential for a healthy attitude is the ability to change our mind.

Whenever we notice our ego gnawing on a grievance, we can simply call time out, then calmly turn our attention to something else. We need not be slaves to our ego. Our mind is under our own control. It is our decision that changes it. And if we make the decision often enough, we find that it becomes a permanent one. A grievance can be banished from our consciousness by repetition. Each time we do it, we remove an obstacle to spiritual progress.

Although his decision to turn his life and will over to the care of God was an important step, says Don, a friend from Los Alamos, it had no real impact on his behavior or attitude until he made a strenuous effort to face, and be rid of, the things in him that had been keeping him from making contact and stunting his spiritual growth. "It was only then that my life took on meaning."

Grievances, of course, erect a wall between us and our Higher Power. A decision not to host a grievance is in the same league with a decision to turn our will over to the care of God as we understand Him. It's a loving decision — one that chooses to accept rather than attack. It's a decision made *with* our Higher Power and *against* our ego. And that works.

7

Negative Feedback

. . . . . .

*There is in all the evil I see
about me some latent germ of good.*

— Barrett Wendell

espite all I can do to rid myself of anger, resentment, envy, greed, malice, mean-spiritedness, despair and the rest of my ego's favorite preoccupations, I'm not likely to see the last of them until I die. Making spiritual progress is about the most I can count on.

That might not be a bad thing. Nowhere does it say we have to be perfect and, in the case of the Third Step, that can work to our advantage.

There is nothing we can do to prevent destructive emotions from popping up. The best retrained ego in the world is going to slip one past us now and then. But we don't have to let anger ruin a friendship or demoralize our family. We don't have to burn with resentment at things we have no control over.

Instead, we can use negative feedback for positive purposes.

Whenever painful, destructive emotions rise to the surface, we are perfectly capable of converting them into an opportunity to get in touch with our Higher Power.

I like to consider every temper flare-up, for instance, as a signal to make another Third Step decision. It never hurts to repeat a decision, and for someone as forgetful as me, it's almost a necessity. I've found that repetition in the pursuit of spiritual progress is always rewarded.

If I find myself wallowing in self-pity, hating someone or inwardly railing at some bizarre twist of fate, it's a sign that I need to take a mental step backward, draw a deep breath and silently say, "Okay, Holy Friend, I'm in trouble again. I need help. My will's not working. How about taking over?"

From sad experience, I know that resisting my character defects only makes them worse. Bad habits dig in their heels when I hitch them up to my willpower. Accepting them, though, does just the opposite. When I acknowledge them, then turn them over to my Higher Power and put them out of my mind, they seem to lose some of their power. It's the best way I know to put the brakes on runaway emotions.

Accept Anger

W.J., an alcoholic from Houston, agrees that anger can't be willed away. He takes it a step further; he says that it must be accepted. Coming from Texas, where everything is bigger, including anger no doubt, he says he even "reacted with anger to the *subject* of anger."

"We couldn't prohibit alcohol by legal proclamation," W.J. says, "and we can't prohibit anger with self-righteous proclamations. Anger is real. It is human. It is a natural emotion. I avoid the word 'normal' because who knows what's normal? Certainly not an alcoholic.

"Am I supposed to lie to myself when I get angry?" W.J. asks. "That's what I did in my drinking days . . . .. I lied to myself. But since I made a decision to turn my will and my life over to the care of God, I can't do that.

"So I get angry and I admit it to myself. Then I have a choice. Isn't that the essence of AA?

"So I can choose not to let my anger burst into rage. Not to let it burn me up with its acid. Not to let it eat my lunch, as we Texans say. I can choose not to let my anger smolder in resentment. I can be 'quick to hear, slow to speak, slow to anger.' I can refuse to let the sun go down on my wrath. I can ponder over how I can possibly 'be angry but sin not.'"

By the time he does all that, W.J. says, his anger is spent, and he's laughing at himself over all the wasted energy and "my own childishness." He's even capable of reaching a profound decision, he says, "such as 'The hell with it!'"

W.J. says he hopes to continue becoming less angry about fewer things. "If not, the only justified anger I dare to have is against myself."[1]

I always have perfectly justifiable reasons for flaring up at someone. Don't we all? But if I examine my reasoning closely, invariably I discover that it's in protection of my ego. It is, in other words, a selfish reaction. Even when I'm angry with someone for hurting someone else, even though I'm genuinely sorry for the victim, my anger really stems from the fact that the offender is insensitive, stupid and vicious. In other words, he or she didn't measure up to *my* moral standards.

I have to admit that all too often I make judgments based purely on what I see rather than on what I know about the offender. When someone does that to me, of course, I'm enraged. How dare someone judge *my* actions that way?

Usually, of course, I don't have time to reason at all. Anger surges up unbidden. But if I don't at least try to wrestle it to the ground, I'm playing God. I'm setting myself up as judge of another person and that's not my role. It's the role of someone who knows far more about that person than I do. Someone like my Higher Power.

Bill W., AA's co-founder, struggled with that problem years ago. "If someone cheats us, aren't we entitled to be mad? Can't we be properly angry with self-righteous folk? For us of AA these are dangerous exceptions. We have found that justified anger ought to be left to those better qualified to handle it."[2]

On the other hand, as *A Course In Miracles* says, "Pardon is *always* justified . . ... If pardon were unjustified, you would be asked to sacrifice your rights when you return forgiveness for attack. But you are merely asked to see forgiveness as the natural reaction to distress that rests on error and thus calls for help. Forgiveness is the only sane response."[3]

But whether we are quick to pardon or not, it is also true that we are never likely to be rid of anger. We are learning what to do when it comes, though. As long as it keeps coming, we can keep using it to our advantage. We can train ourselves to "Think Higher Power" every time it surfaces and make another decision to turn our will over. That's the most useful justification for anger.

One reason we want to be free of anger, not to mention all our other negative emotions, is that it makes us miserable. Only when we are able to turn our will over to our Higher Power do we find relief.

The reality of the situation, though, is that negative emotions will continue dogging us as long as we need them. And we do need them. Without these feelings, the outbursts they trigger, the people they hurt, the personal pain and remorse they bring — how would we know what needs healing?

That's especially true of people whose family situations have created fear and guilt, people who have suffered mental and physical violence, people who have stuffed their anger for years — so long that it has become both habitual and unconscious. These injured feelings can't be healed until they are out in the open, so that when our anger erupts, we need not deny or be ashamed of it. We only need to know that help is available.

We reach our Maker sometimes through great pain. Though we may howl at the injustice of it, we make progress through acceptance, not resistance. Suffering is temporary. So are all losses and failures to reach the marks we set for ourselves. We need to remind ourselves of that and of the fact that all of these negative influences, as painful and demoralizing as they are at first, can turn out to be useful.

Although negativity is not a place to *stay*, it can rekindle our zeal for inner work. It can get us off of zero when nothing else seems able to. Then we must let go and let our Higher Power manage the progress. Letting go and letting God — that's the essence of the Third Step. We can be grateful that we get there through negative feedback as well as positive.

8

Accentuate The Positive

. . . . . .

By often repeating these acts,
they become habitual and the presence
of God rendered as it were
natural to us.

— Brother Lawrence

commitment isn't worth much if we invest nothing in it. We can back into it, that's true. We've seen that. We can be pushed and shoved into it by pain and failure. We can be pulled into it, kicking and screaming at the injustice. But at some point we have to use our own volition. At some point we have to say, and mean it, "This is my choice. This is what I want." When we do that, something changes.

It changes even faster when we actively partic- ipate in this commitment. We have made a deci- sion to turn our will and our lives over to a Higher Power. Now we need to reinforce that decision by structuring our day to make room for our Higher Power. We need somehow to make sure that whatever it is we do, we do together; whatever decisions we make, we make jointly. Our Higher Power needs to be included in our daily tasks so that we do not forget the source of our growing confidence.

There are many ways to do this, and the simple ones, the practical ones, the common, everyday, garden-variety ones are probably those that work best for us individually. They are the easiest to remember and surely the easiest to begin. These are ways simply to cultivate companionship with our Higher Power. They don't need to be elaborate or complicated; they just need to be convenient and workable.

For instance, when I start my day with a cup of coffee, I can say a short prayer with the first sip. Coffee-with-a-prayer is a good eye-opener. I like to say something like this:

"Good morning, HP. Thanks for the sleep and a clear head. What have you got in store for us today? Help me not to get into anything that the two of us can't get out of. Make me useful today, okay? Amen."

The day is full of opportunities to make contact. All of us have certain things that we do every day pretty much on schedule. To stay in touch with our Higher Power, we can pick out a few of these as reminders to ask for guidance or to say thanks.

Here are a few ordinary routine things we might do every day, each of which we could use as a point of spiritual reference:

Let out the cat or walk the dog.
Brush our teeth.
Comb our hair.
Milk the cow.
Eat breakfast.
Read the paper.
Start the car.
Call sponsor, sponsee or both.
Open the mail.
Do the crossword puzzle.
Compose today's action plan.
Smile at a co-worker.
File a report.
Another helping of coffee (juice, soda, etc.).
Have lunch.
Similar afternoon routines.
Punch the clock.
Eat supper.
Go to a meeting.
Write a letter.

Watch the news.

Read a book or take in a movie.

Go to bed — but not before a thank-you prayer and a Tenth-Step review!

At any time of day, of course, we can reach into a pocket and rub the poker chip or medallion that we were given in our 12-Step group, a perfect reminder that we have not come this far alone.

One-Minute Contact With Our Higher Power

It's easy. Make your own list of things you do every day, then choose those that lend themselves to a moment of reflection, a plea for help, a quick thank you.

A one-minute contact with our Higher Power in the middle of a busy day is a better pick-me-up than a candy bar, a health-food snack or a jolt of caffeine. And one minute is enough.

Kenneth Blanchard and Spencer Johnson wrote a business bestseller called *The One Minute Manager.* Its message is that managing people is not complicated but simple, that it requires very little time. Managers are taught to teach their employees to set clear goals that take no more than a minute to review. They agree on the goals and go over them often to compare performance with the goal. In each case, a minute is all it takes.

It takes no more than a minute to do the same with our Higher Power. Throughout the day we can review our behavior to see if it matches our goals, and ask for help in making adjustments.

The key to success is to make it habit-forming. Our one-minute contacts with our Higher Power will be more effective if linked to actions so habitual that they are automatic, the things we are so accustomed to doing every day that we don't give them a thought. Now we *do* want to start giving these automatic actions a thought — a one-minute thought. Each time we start to do them can be a signal to make contact with God. We need to commit ourselves to paying attention every time we drink that cup of coffee or push the elevator button or feed the chickens.

It's important for me to make contact before — not during or after — I read the mail. A typical day finds me dealing with a lot of people and working under deadline pressure. It's hard for me to take time out to minister to my inner needs. I have to remind myself about priorities. But for my Higher Power, I might not even have a job. Can I afford to ignore this Friend? Surely, I can postpone for one minute whatever it is I have to do. I can let the mail go unread. Some of it took days to arrive. What's another minute? Besides, if I wait until after I read that tantalizing letter from my rich uncle Harry, I may never get back to my Higher Power. A serious interruption of my routine is much more likely to occur if I don't put first things first.

Putting our Higher Power first is a good spiritual habit to get into. If the morning paper is to be a contact signal, the news can wait. Finding out what our Higher Power would like us to do this day is more important than last night's ball scores or a report on the tipsy stock market or a story about how much more our taxes are going up.

But let's be reasonable about this, too. There are some parts of our daily routine that are more demanding than others. Not to mention that *some* days are more demanding than others. Before the Battle of Edgehill, Sir Jacob Astley was said to have uttered this prayer: "Oh Lord, Thou knowest how busy I must be this day. If I forget thee, do not thou forget me."[1]

If we choose a God-related reminder that can be inconvenient to postpone for a minute or one loaded with potential complications, anxiety may eat into the minute with our Higher Power. That will only defeat its purpose. We ought to discard the idea of using any activity that is likely to be consistently inconvenient or upsetting. It'll be more trouble than it's worth.

For instance, if we choose seeing the kids off to school as our trigger for a contact, we're liable to hear, "I can't find my book!" more often than the voice of our Higher Power.

In choosing our contact reminders, we need to prepare for contingencies and be realistic about possible conflicts. It may save us from getting discouraged. A few routine actions that are well chosen will serve us better than a dozen or more ill-considered ones.

If weaving our contacts with our Higher Power into our daily routines doesn't work for everyone — and it won't for everyone — there are other things we can do.

Breath Prayers

Some people repeat "Thy will be done" as often as possible throughout the day. I do it myself. Brief as it is, that's a contact worth making. Some silently say the Serenity Prayer whenever they get a chance:

> God grant me the serenity to accept the things I cannot change,
> Courage to change the things I can, and
> The wisdom to know the difference.

We may not always feel like doing any of these things. But as Mary McDermott Shideler, past president of the American Theological Society, says, "Going through the motions has its place in spirituality as much as in love."[2]

Whatever it is we choose to remind ourselves of our Creator, it will be something, ideally, that does not interfere with our daily work. Our one-minute spirituality breaks will make all the difference to us, but not a difference the casual observer can see. Except, that is, in our resulting calmer attitudes. The more we do it, the calmer we're apt to become. Repetition is the key.

For B.C., a Canadian friend, "The Second and Third Steps seemed an insurmountable obstacle to the rest of the Steps." He struggled through two years in AA, "constantly plagued by the desire to drink." Then one day, at a family reunion, he was struck by the realization that the compulsion to drink had left him.

"It was some kind of miracle for me, for I knew I had done nothing to rid myself of that compulsion," B.C. says.

"I hadn't asked any 'Higher Power' to help me. The nearest I had come to praying was to repeat the Serenity Prayer with others at meetings. Could this be it? Could this single prayer, repeated at meeting after meeting without conviction on my part, have done it? This had to be the answer. Others at those meetings were not as reluctant as I. Perhaps their simple sincerity lent some validity to my repeating the prayer with them.

"This is what I came to believe," says B.C. "Their belief was more powerful than my unbelief."[3]

A simple prayer, repeated over and over — anyone can do that. Without an appointment. Without believing anything will happen. It's progress.

We can stop during the day whenever we find an appropriate occasion and find a place to be alone for a few minutes at a time. Maybe on a coffee break or at lunchtime. Maybe during a walk around the block or a trip to the rest room. Wherever or whenever, it can be our period of solitude, a little time with our Higher Power. Two or three of these longer intermissions during the day, unhurried and uninterrupted, can equal a whole bunch of one-minute contacts.

If we're in a position to do it, taking unscheduled breaks can be just as rewarding, and possibly more exciting. For instance, say we're in the middle of a nerve-racking conversation with fellow workers. Or maybe there's a hot sales conference going on and we're jittery. We stand up, say, "Excuse me," and step outside for a moment. There we quickly examine the way we feel. If it's not a feeling of comfort and confidence, we ask our Higher Power to show us what's wrong. Maybe we'll discover that we're uptight about impressing our fellow workers or our boss. Maybe we'll think no one appreciates our efforts. If we're lucky, maybe we'll flash to the fact that we're investing our emotions in something that is of no real value, that we are too intent on acquiring wealth, power or prestige — none of which can bring us happiness.

We think about that, then return to our meeting, spirits restored, values in place.

We can make contact with our Higher Power, of course, any time we please. It need not be a planned, structured thing.

Taking a deep breath can be a spiritual reminder as we breathe in peace and let out frustrations.

We can close our eyes and visualize loving friends.

We can think of our Higher Power every time we see the color green.

We can make a connection with our Source in the eyes of a laughing child, in the rosy glow of a sunrise, in the boom of thunder on a stormy night, in the thrashing beak of a hungry pelican.

All we have to do is be alert to the presence of God as we understand Him, and there is nowhere we cannot meet.

My Higher Power hurled into the sky an inextinguishable ball of fire with as little effort as it took to make a blade of grass. My Higher Power devoted as much painstaking detail to the creation of a mallard duck as to the composition of the universe. My Higher Power cares as much for sots and sluts as for popes and presidents. When I see this evidence of a loving Creator and realize that I can arrange a meeting at any time of the day, I wonder why I find it so hard to work God into my schedule. What else is more important?

When I make time for my Higher Power, my Higher Power spends time with me.

9

Look Who's Talking
To God

. . . . . .

*The purpose of all prayer
is to find God's will and to make
that will our prayer.*

— Catherine Marshall

W e've seen the need to turn our will over, we've made a commitment to do it and we've begun daily to make room for our Higher Power. Now some of us are getting cold feet. We find that we're not too comfortable making contact. How do we approach our Higher Power? How do we strike up a conversation? Or know what to ask for, or whether we should ask at all? What *is* this thing called prayer, and how do we go about it? Do we even know what it *means* to pray?

"A few years ago, I was asked by a friend what it meant to be human," says therapist and teacher Silvio E. Fittipaldi. "The only response I could think of at the time was, 'The fact that you ask that question is what it means to be human.' I would add now that this is what it means to pray. It means to go below the surface of life. It means to live from one's depth, without losing touch with the surface of life. What takes place at the surface has depth at its heart, and one can live truly at the surface by living from that depth."[1]

As a child, I was introduced to prayer by my mother. She taught my brothers and me to kneel beside the bed and recite, "Now I lay me down to sleep, I pray the Lord my soul to keep. If I should die before I wake, I pray the Lord my soul to take."

71

Kneeling wasn't required, but the prayer was. Later I
learned the Lord's Prayer, the one that's used now to close
many of our 12-Step meetings, and others of my own
making. Before I reached adulthood, though, I had quit
praying. For many years I had no use for anything
religious. I doubted the existence of God. If I were to
pray, this is the only thing I would have asked: "What the
hell have you got against me?"

That's hardly the kind of prayer for doing the Third
Step. But it's a start. It's a door opener. Remember, it says
we "made a decision to turn our will and our lives over to
the care of God *as we understood Him."* Maybe a question
like, "What have you got against me?" is appropriate. It's
certainly going to take more than, "Now I lay me down to
sleep" and the Lord's Prayer, recited by rote, to begin to
understand H.P.

The Nature Of Prayer

There may be as many ideas about how to pray as there
are prayers. Can a prayer that is read or recited, for instance, be a channel to our Maker? Is a sincere, straight-
from-the-heart appeal, however fumbling and crude, as
welcome as one that comes from a prayer book?

My notion is that a sincere, conscious, purposeful, one-
on-one approach can hardly go wrong. As a matter of
fact, it is the only way a lot of us are likely to discover
with what or whom we are making contact.

"Prayer should be understood, not as a mere mechanical
recitation of formulas, but as a mystical elevation, an ab-
sorption of consciousness in the contemplation of a principle both permeating and transcending our world," said
Nobel laureate Alexis Carrel, the French surgeon and bi-
ologist. "Such a psychological state is not intellectual. It is
incomprehensible to philosophers and scientists, and inac-
cessible to them. But the simple seem to feel God as easily
as the heat of the sun or the kindness of a friend."[2]

Prayer, in its broadest sense, is a way of coming to
understand HP. It is more than what the dictionary de-

fines as entreaty or offering. In its broadest sense, it includes meditation, contemplation, devotion, intercession,
wonder, instruction (yes, notice how often we catch ourselves *telling* HP what to do for us?) and other forms of
interaction with a power greater than ourselves. Much of
it is simply questioning.

Prayer Questions

Nobel laureate Elie Wiesel, in his personal memoir *Night*,
asked "Why did I pray?" and heard his teacher Moshe say,
"Man raises himself toward God by the questions he asks
him. . .. That is true dialogue. Man questions and God
answers. But we don't understand his answers. We can't
understand them because they come from the depths of
the soul, and they stay there until death."[3]

How can questions raise a person to God? Why even
want to be raised to God?

A follower asks his Hindu guru, "Why do you always
answer my questions with a question?" And his guru
replies, "Do I?"

Fittipaldi dares to answer: "A question asked is an
opening of one's self. When I ask a question, I open myself to something 'other' than the usual and even 'other'
than myself. To ask a question is to realize that I have
some input into that very situation in which the question
is posed."[4]

Fittipaldi means that a person and his question are not
separate. Nor can the petitioner be apart from his prayer.
The one who prays makes himself part of God's answer.

This, of course, answers both the how and the why of
being raised to God.

Some of our discussion of prayer is oriented toward the
Judeo-Christian tradition but nothing said here is intended
to persuade anyone to follow that path. Twelve-Step programs are spiritual in nature and spirituality is not necessarily based on any particular religious tradition or form
of worship. But when prayer is found within any religious
tradition, it is always an attempt to approach the source

of that body of beliefs. That is what we are trying to do
— approach our Source.

Many of us who sense a stirring, an urging, a hunger
beyond bodily appetites, beyond the familiar five senses,
may not believe in a deity and are, in fact, offended at the
suggestion that we must believe in one if we are to get
what our program offers. Humanists are as capable of
giving and receiving love as anyone, and love of course is
the keystone of our recovery. We should feel free to inter-
pret references to a Higher Power or God any way that's
meaningful to us — as transcendent love, ultimate reality
or perhaps something else that makes sense and feels
spiritually comfortable.

A skeptical AA member asked another who had been
heard to voice similar doubts why she bothered to pray.
"How can you pray to someone who isn't there?"

"Someone's there, all right," the other skeptic said. "I
am. Maybe Someone else is too. I'm not sure. But when I
pray for what I need to know, my prayers are somehow
answered. I don't know if it's a force outside of me or
whether I'm tapping some power within. But something is
getting through to me."

"There's only one prerequisite," says French philosopher
Edouard LeRoy. "One condition has to be met. The decision must be taken in advance not only in words but in
reality to say yes to the light. This attitude is called prayer.
In fact, it is prayer even before we realize that we should
call it so."

LeRoy believes that the only search for God is through
prayer, but "not through the formulas of ritual." He suggests, instead, a prayer like this:

"I am nothing. I know nothing, save the fact that I am
here, full of need and misery, full of ignorance, doubt and
fear. But I am finding my direction. I turn inward toward
an ideal of higher, purer spirituality. I will the good, even
the good unknown to me. I aspire and trust. I crave. I
open myself. I abandon myself to the God whose inspira-
tion I feel at work in the depths of myself. I will the light.

I call upon it. I am confident that it will answer me and I accept in advance everything that it will exact from me."[5]

Many of us are beginners at prayer. We often feel like neophytes even if we have been going through the motions for years. As beginners, we don't yet know what possibilities prayer offers. We don't know what our capabilities are nor do we know the limits of prayer, if limits there are.

But this uncertainty is not confined to novices. François Fénelon (1651-1715), French theologian and Archbishop of Cambrai — a man who should have known something about addressing God — voiced the same uncertainty. "Lord, I know not what I ought to ask of Thee. Thou only knowest what I need . . . behold my needs which I know not myself . . . I would have no other desire than to accomplish Thy will. Teach me to pray. Pray Thyself in me."

"Pray Thyself in me" — which of us at some point has not wanted our Higher Power to take the initiative?

". . . The essence of prayer is not a mystical lifting up of the mind to God but the descent of the Spirit into our hearts," says Donald Bloesch. "It is not climbing the mystical ladder to heaven but taking hold of the outstretched hand of God."[6]

How Should We Pray?

We approach God not knowing what to do or say or even what attitude to carry into our prayers. Shall we prostrate ourselves, physically or figuratively? Shall we take the arm-around-the-shoulders approach, buddy to buddy? Do we dare regard our Higher Power as our lover and try to reciprocate?

This is something we have to figure out for ourselves with God's help. It is between us and our inner guide. Being a private intimate thing, we have no reason just to take someone's word for it. If anything calls for experimentation, this does. We all arrived here on different paths. Our genetic inheritance, our upbringing, our education and our life experiences are not identical. They combine to make the spiritual approach of each of us a little different from that of our fellows. Why then should we feel that we must shoehorn ourselves into someone else's pattern of prayer or that of a particular religious system? Someone else's way may not be for us.

Some people feel natural approaching God on a casual conversational level, as a friend to whom to turn throughout the day, getting consistent moral support in that way. Some can't. Some can approach God only with reverence and veneration, with a sense of awe that befits the exalted position of Supreme Leader.

A Course In Miracles sees our relationship with God as warm and personal. "He asks no more than that He hear you call Him 'Friend'."[7]

However we choose to make the approach, though, is less important than that we do. Each of us must somehow develop a working relationship with God — and with our fellow human beings as well, for they are a vital part of our spiritual lives.

Our 12-Step program shows us that the people in our fellowship and throughout our daily lives are indispensable to any spiritual progress we may make. It follows that they are just as indispensable in prayer. Many of us have felt that God was speaking to us through something that a friend or sometimes a stranger had to say.

In the beginning, of course, prayer is always for ourselves. As children, our first impulse to pray was self-protective. It still is. We are afraid. We want safety. We want health. We want our loved ones to be safe and healthy so that we won't be left alone. We want our enemies satisfied so that they won't be tempted to harm us. We want possessions, comfort, the good opinion of others and the ability to exercise some control over others.

We may pray for these things, if only subliminally. And though these wishes are essentially selfish, that's not necessarily bad. No prayer is to be scorned. Every prayer, after all, puts us in touch with our Higher Power.

And each prayer remains an individual action. It is one of those things we must do for ourselves, regardless of how we do it.

G.K. Chesterton points out that there are some "things we do not wish a man to do at all unless he does them well," such as brain surgery or running a restaurant. On the other hand, there are "things we want a man to do for himself, even if he does them badly," he says, such as, "writing one's own love letters or blowing one's own nose."[8]

And we now must add, praying one's own prayers.

We can take comfort in the fact that we will not be given a test. We will not be graded. In fact, except perhaps in the eyes of the holier-than-thou, we cannot pray badly at all.

"We can differentiate types, but not qualities, of worship, as the prayer of intercession from the prayer of thanksgiving," says Mary McDermott Shideler, "but not 'foolish devotions' from those that are not foolish."[9]

Prayer, whether we think we've done it well or poorly, also lends perspective.

"How the hell am I going to take myself so seriously if I'm on my knees praying?" said Edwin, a dually addicted alcoholic in a Third Step discussion. "It's when I'm up there in the clouds thinking I know everything that I have problems."

Prayer is useful in bringing us closer to others, too. If a prayer is on behalf of another, for instance, it unites us with that person. We are spiritually joined with anyone we focus on in our prayers. They become a part of us. Can we pray for anyone without helping ourselves?

We Are Not Alone

Although our prayers ultimately are for ourselves, we can no more get answers for ourselves alone than we can find happiness alone. God speaks to us through other people — through what they say, what they do and how they interact with us. In one way or another, our answers usually come from others. That's because each one is our equal, each is loved as we are, each has the capacity to think our thoughts and feel what we are feeling. We are truly one. We cannot hear our Higher Power's voice alone because we are not alone. Our spiritual condition at any given moment is the product of our relationship with others.

Are we being hard on them? Then we are being hard on ourselves. Criticism of another always comes back to us. Our desire to help another does too. It helps us, it calms and soothes us. Any sense of fulfillment that we may feel usually has something to do with others. That should tell us something about prayer.

Try to go to sleep while concentrating on yourself. It is impossible. Self-absorption is the enemy of sleep. But if we allow our mind to drift, to survey the human landscape and to focus on other people doing other things, it begins to entertain us and sleep comes.

It is the same with prayer. Self-absorption is the enemy of prayer, of contact with our Higher Power. But if we allow our inner nature, our natural feelings of goodwill toward others to take over, we quickly find ourselves in harmony with our Higher Power. We are at that moment in communion with God.

Our Eleventh Step suggests that we pray "only for knowledge of His will for us and the power to carry it out." I try to do that, although I find myself also praying for specific things or specific people. Sometimes I'm able to forget the specifics and let all of my desires go into God's hands. It's my way of saying I trust God. And peace comes. Do I want to trade this for a bit of trifling advice about a problem that I may not even remember in a week or a month or a year? God takes care of me. I don't need to tell Him how.

Finally, there is really nothing to do as we approach our Source but to try to get out of the way.

"If the experts agree on one essential quality of mind and heart, in this work of practicing the presence of God in prayer, that essential is humility," says Elizabeth Hunter in the anthology, *The Choice Is Always Ours.* "For say they all, the real work of prayer is done by God — our part is to empty the heart of those things which keep Him out."[10]

10

Tricking The Mind

. . . . . .

*If we have not quiet in
our minds, outward comfort will do no
more for us than a golden slipper
on a gouty foot.*

— John Bunyan

Tere are many ways to practice meditation, but there is only one purpose for me: to step out of the way, to yield to my Higher Power.

I'm too full of myself. I think too much, mostly about myself — what the world owes me, how badly I'm treated and who is to blame. My ego is busy-busy-busy. So I need to slow the mind, banish the words, muffle the thoughts and shift from drive into neutral. My idea of meditation is to become still.

In that quieted state, when the mental chatter has slowed to a murmur, I can relax. I can begin to hear not my ego but my spiritual guide.

My ego, though, does everything it can to thwart me. It doesn't want to lose control. And loss of control is exactly what is supposed to happen in this deep state of relaxation. To prevent it, my ego frantically calls to mind upsetting thoughts. Its purpose is to stir up my feelings, while *my* purpose is to calm them so that I can meditate unhampered by emotional distractions.

The Power Of Meditation

As an alcoholic, I need all the tools this program offers, including the two in Step Eleven — prayer

and meditation. But unlike prayer, meditation isn't something to *do*. Sometimes the more we try to do, the less
likely we are to succeed. Meditation often happens when
we're doing something else. It isn't the practice of a mental
or physical technique, although a technique is useful in
reaching the state of nondoing that we call meditation.

Meditation has been around a long time and is honored
all over the world. Writing in the 14th Century, an anonymous Christian monk said that he had developed his
own contemplative techniques and that each meditator
needed to find what was best for himself.

"And if you think that the labor is great, then you may
seek to develop special ways, tricks, private techniques
and spiritual devices by means of which you can put other
thoughts away. It is best to learn these methods from
God by your own experience rather than from any man in
this life. Although this is so, I will tell you what seems to
me to be the best of these special ways. Test them and
improve upon them if you can."

This monk advised trying to cover one's thoughts "with
a thick cloud of forgetting as though they never existed
neither for you nor for any other man. And if they continue to arise, continue to put them down."

One of his "tricks" was to choose a word or name of a
single syllable, such as "God" or "love." "Or if you like,
choose another that suits your tastes, provided that it is
of one syllable. Clasp this word tightly in your heart so
that it never leaves it no matter what may happen. This
word shall be your shield and your spear whether you
ride in peace or in war. With this word you shall beat
upon the cloud and the darkness, which are above you.
With this word you shall strike down thoughts of every
kind and drive them beneath the cloud of forgetting."[1]

Most of us automatically use something like the "cloud
of forgetting" all the time. How often have we driven our
car over a familiar route while deep in thought and arrived
at our destination without thinking of turns we had made
or traffic lights we had obeyed? We can put a part of our

mind into neutral whenever we choose. If the doorbell rings while we're reading, we absent-mindedly lay down the magazine and return to it later, picking up the thread where we left off. We can do the same in meditation, taking time out to tune in to our inner guide and picking up the thread of our activities later. And vice versa. We can flip our mental toggle switch whenever it's appropriate.

Meditation Techniques

Martin Luther in 1534 said that seekers after God could prevent thoughts from intruding on their quiet time by achieving a passive attitude. This was done, he said, by dwelling on an object that would let "the heart free itself and become joyous." Luther suggested concentrating on the words of the Lord's Prayer, the Ten Commandments, the Psalms and a number of the recorded sayings of Christ or the Apostle Paul.

This attitude finds parallels in our 12-Step program. For instance, it came to an addict in Fort Myers Beach, Florida, to meditate on the "fruits of our program." This, he says, was easy, "for they are countless. I can choose a new topic every time I meditate — things like love, honesty, humility, faith, compassion, happiness, willingness, gratitude, tolerance, truth, hope, open-mindedness, trust and serenity. Meditation, in fact, is an opportunity for me to appreciate all over again all the blessings of our fellowship."

Our program appeals to the mathematical mind of an engineer named Tom. He says he is in the process of showing scientifically that the more he puts into his spiritual discipline, the more he receives. Tom says that meditation in particular yields peace of mind and that the 12 Steps are helpful in getting him into a meditative mood.

He starts out "by going from 1 through 12 and briefly checking where I am." Then he focuses on a phrase such as "God, grant me serenity," "Surrender brings faith," "Thy will be done" or "God is love." As his thoughts stray, he keeps bringing them back to the theme he has chosen until his mind slows. Eventually, he says, his wandering thoughts are replaced by peace, calm and a sense of direction.

Another 12 Stepper, serving in the Army in India, assigned key words to each Step, such as these:

Step One	— powerlessness
Step Two	— sanity
Step Three	— God
Step Four	— inventory
Step Five	— admission
Step Six	— readiness
Step Seven	— humility
Step Eight	— list
Step Nine	— amends
Step Ten	— spot-check
Step Eleven	— prayer
Step Twelve	— message

"Soon," he said, "it was easy to recall every beautiful and meaningful word in every Step. I would then meditate on one at a time and try to review my day in light of that Step. The Higher Power certainly worked for me in keeping out extraneous thoughts. Within the first week, I found that I could meditate on my spiritual progress and gain new insight into my implementation of the Steps in my daily life. I now find that a deep inner peace suffuses my being as I carry out this meditation."[2]

Others feel that, instead of focusing on a word or an inspiring phrase, it is necessary to empty the mind of all thoughts. In many spiritual traditions, the aim is to make the mind a void so that any message from the Higher Power is not confused with the ego's demands. Sometimes we empty the mind unintentionally and spontaneously as when we stand contemplating a sunset over the water.

A word or phrase that we repeat over and over is meant to lull us away from our ordinary thoughts. The word can be full of meaning for us, as are those that have been suggested, or the word can be free of any special significance.

For instance, in Transcendental Meditation, a Yogic technique for achieving a higher consciousness, a trained instructor gives the student a *mantra* — a secret word or sound or phrase — which the student promises not to divulge. The purpose of focusing on the word and repeating it to the point of boredom is to prevent distracting thoughts.

Boredom is the very thing that's needed, in fact, because it takes our mind away from our purpose. If we try to *think* our way into meditation, some of us may never enter. The thinking part of us resists it. But can we do *anything* without thinking? Yes, we can if we have a device to distract our mind — to lull it to sleep, as it were. We think about the device, such as the repetition of a word, and our mind is put off guard.

Meditation is a passage into the unknown. As soon as we approach uncharted waters, our mind raises the alarm. Since an alarm hinders meditation, we need a device to draw our attention away. One device, of course, is the mantra. Saying a mantra over and over will eventually push us across the line, nudging us gently into the unknown, a sort of twilight reverie where our minds are unaccustomed to taking us.

Another way of entering this twilight zone involves the practice of inducing low-frequency brain-wave control. It usually involves some kind of countdown, concentrating on seeing the indicator on a scale or meter moving from a high number to lower numbers, or imagining yourself slowly descending a set of stairs. The slowed state of mental activity in which the brain is producing low-frequency alpha waves supposedly is the ideal condition for getting in touch with one's deepest spiritual resources. Alpha waves have been recorded in both Yoga and Zen meditators.

Ecumenical Techniques From Past Ages

While many spiritual traditions teach specific ways of inducing the state of mind that permits the crossover into the unknown, most share certain techniques. Here is a generic method of creating the meditative reverie, a sort of composite of techniques recorded down through the ages:

1. Choose a time of day and a place where you will not be interrupted and where there will be a minimum of noise or distracting sounds of any kind.

2. Sit upright in a comfortable position on a chair with both feet flat on the floor or in the cross-legged lotus position, either on pillows or the floor. Using the techniques while lying down will induce sleep.

3. Keep your eyes closed, unless you are using a gazing technique such as staring at a candle flame.

4. Consciously relax all muscles, beginning at your feet and moving up to your head, thinking how soft and limber each set of muscles has become. Keep them relaxed.

5. Breathe naturally, through your nose if possible. Pay attention to your breathing. Be conscious of each inhalation and exhalation. As you breathe out, say a one-syllable word of your choosing, such as "peace," "God," "love" or any other one that feels good or appropriate. Repeat the word or name silently each time you breathe out. Continue to breathe easily and naturally.

6. When distracting thoughts come to mind, do not fight them. Accept the fact that they will come. When they do, simply dismiss them and return your attention to your breathing and the repetition of your mental device.

7. Keep this up for 15 or 20 minutes. You can check the time, but don't use an alarm. Allow enough time at the outset not to be anxious about the time.

8. When time is up, stay seated for several minutes, at first with eyes closed and later open.

9. Tell yourself that each session is a success, regardless of how well you were able to keep extraneous thoughts from interfering. Don't worry if you don't feel deeply relaxed the first few times. It will come.

10. Practice once or twice daily, and always either before meals or before bedtime, never directly following a meal.

The methods of Transcendental Meditation and other disciplines for inducing the meditative state have been scientifically tested at the Thorndike Memorial Laboratory of Harvard, showing that, "Any sound or phrase or prayer or mantra brings forth the same physiologic changes."

"In other words," says Dr. Herbert Benson, who directed the project, "using the basic necessary components, any of the age-old or the newly derived techniques produces the same physiologic results regardless of the mental device used."[3]

Meditative Practices

Another means of taking the leap into the unknown is to keep a personal journal, a diary or a daily log — something I've enjoyed experimenting with. Journaling for me involves recording not just events but my thoughts and emotions. The simple act of taking pen in hand and beginning to jot down thoughts has brought surprising results. The writing itself helps to still my mind and focus it, dispelling mental chatter, so that, in the words of Chinese philosopher Lao-Tzu, "Muddy water, let stand, becomes clear."

In my journaling, I have had an imaginary dialogue with people who have helped shape my life, reviewing the events that have most affected me and so on. Mostly, though, I just set out my thoughts as they come to me. However it's done, journaling tends to take on a purpose of its own and puts one in touch with inner resources previously unknown. At least it did for me.

Zen teachers use the koan way of finding the "unknown." Koans are insolvable puzzles. Reason is of little use, although it first appears that the riddle will yield to logic. So the student is enticed to think about it. "What is the sound of one hand clapping?" The mind goes to work on it. Somewhere, somehow, a soundless sound can be found, can it not? Eventually, the mind's effort collapses like a flat tire. The trained mind has given out; the student has become a child receptive to the "unknown."

In many religions and cultures, revelations are said to come to people in a trance. Sufi dervishes, members of a Muslim religious order, for some 700 years have used dance for that purpose. These "whirling dervishes" spin until they reach a trancelike state, when the dance becomes mindless.

A shaman, or holy man, is a focal point of tribal religions in many parts of the world. The shaman is supposed to be able to go into a trance at will. The song or chant intoned by a shaman brings on a trance or calm state of mind not unfamiliar to the self-induced states of mind in Christian, Jewish, Yogic, Buddhist, Taoist and other traditions, some of whom also use gazing and rhythmic breathing techniques. Sharing the practice of trance-inducing chanting are aborigines of Australia, tribes of Siberia and Native Americans. These are not unlike some charismatic religious practices in modern America.

As we see, it's common among the world's spiritual traditions to journey within to the silent reaches of individual consciousness and experience what many say is a peace that is not attainable in ordinary living.

In every meditative practice, the idea is to take our minds from the outer world of sight and sound to an inner world where we can get in touch with what some would call our true being. William James, known as the father of modern psychology, believed that, "The visible world is part of a more spiritual universe from which it draws its chief significance; that union or harmonious relation with that higher universe is our true end; that prayer or inner communion with the spirit thereof — be that spirit 'God' or 'law' — is a process wherein work is really done, and spiritual energy flows in and produces effects, psychological or material within the phenomenal world."[4]

Meditation, then, is the doorway to an unknown self or a window on the soul. Within each of us is something that escapes our understanding. It is the essence of our being, the source of our highest ideals, where our reserves of love and peace are stored. We can reach it by tricking our ego into dropping its guard, by lulling it into inattention. Those who make a practice of this on a regular basis swear by it.

One of our fellowship has observed, "As considerable time passed, I learned that when we stop struggling for what we think we want, then and then only, we begin to get what we *really* want. To me, this does not mean praying for specifics. It simply means spending time each day using a phrase or a word that helps keep my thoughts turned to God. In my experience, there is a definite correlation between the amount of time spent in meditation and the degree of change.

"The quantity of meditation *does* influence the quality. If I double the amount of time spent in meditation, it seems to me that the results are not twice as good, but four times as good. It all comes from consistent practice and has nothing to do with talking, reading or studying."[5]

Marge, a program veteran in Atlanta, has developed the habit of starting her day with meditation that includes looking at herself "through God's eyes and accepting what I see."

Meditation: it's not a bad way of looking at things.

11

What's That I Hear?

. . . . . .

It is the province of knowledge to speak and it is the privilege of wisdom to listen.

— Oliver Wendell Holmes

ot everyone can reach a deep meditative state. I haven't been consistently successful. At times I seem to lack the patience or the ability to focus on an object or thought that will open a window on the soul. Maybe I just don't take to the idea. There's an inner resistance. Whatever it is, the muddied water never seems to clear entirely. Others have told me the same thing. But we needn't despair.

Although many may consistently establish contact with their Higher Power through one or more of the various disciplines of meditation, some of us will always have difficulty putting our minds into neutral.

But we make contact with our Higher Power in other ways. It can be done just by being alert to everything that's going on around us. I hear my Inner Guide in the voice of a stranger, the wording of a billboard, the laughter of a child or the cooing of a dove. All I have to do is listen.

Many of us hear it in a group setting. Our 12-Step discussion meetings provide the occasion and the setting for a contact just as sure, just as meaningful and just as inspiring as any we might receive in silent contemplation at home or in a place of worship. If we can quit worrying about what we are going to say in these discussions, and listen closely to what our hearts and others are saying, something more than earthly voices enters our consciousness.

Within a group of like-minded people who meet together over a long period of time, we begin sharing personal feelings and experiences. We tend to drop our shields. Our ego defenses fall. As we become more open to one another, we also become more open to the psychic domain in general, what many of us would call the spirit of love that permeates these discussions. It opens us to deeper levels of ourselves and to the spiritual world beyond our everyday understanding. Few would deny that we who take part are in touch with spiritual guidance.

Guidance can also be heard alone simply by listening. All it takes is cultivating a receptive attitude. We pick a quiet moment and still our minds, not fighting extraneous thoughts but just letting them drift by. Guidance comes if we listen.

The Oxford Group Approach

The man responsible for developing the spiritual approach that attracted the founders of Alcoholics Anonymous, the first 12-Step program, was a confirmed listener. As a matter of fact, Frank Buchman, founder of the Oxford Group, turned listening into something of an art. For most of his life he did nothing without inner guidance. He had no complicated formula for preparing himself to receive that guidance. He just sat up in bed in the silence of the early morning and, with pen and paper in hand, intently listened.

Buchman himself had been influenced by Professor Henry Wright of Yale, whose book, *The Will of God and A Man's Lifework*, was published in 1909. The theme of Wright's book was that anyone, listening for guidance, could find direction for daily living. Wright set aside a half hour each morning for a "two-way prayer" — listening as well as talking. He daily wrote down what he called "luminous thoughts" in a notebook and tried to act on them. Buchman did the same.

Buchman looked upon a daily period of listening, which he and his followers called their "quiet time," as "an unhurried time when God can really have a chance to imprint His thoughts in your mind." It was his contention that "adequate, accurate information can come from the mind of God to the mind of man."

Every morning, at five o'clock or earlier, Buchman was awake "and conscious of the presence of God. Some days it is simply a series of luminous thoughts of things God wants me to do that day. Some days it is just a sense of peace and rest and one or two outstanding things. Other days it is a sense of need for intercession on behalf of certain people. It takes all the fret, strain and worry out of life."[1]

Because of the human proclivity for self-deception, Buchman was aware that not every thought that came into his mind was divinely inspired. Some of the world's great despots have been convinced they were doing the will of God. To guard against grandiosity, Buchman urged his followers to ask themselves if the guidance they felt they had received met their highest personal standards of honesty, purity, unselfishness and love. He also urged them to get the advice of friends who were also trying to live by God's guidance.

This precaution was not lost on Bill W. "Going it alone in spiritual matters is dangerous," he wrote. "How many times have we heard well-intentioned people claim the guidance of God when it was all too plain that they were sorely mistaken? Lacking both practice and humility, they had deluded themselves and were able to justify the most arrant nonsense on the ground that this was what God had told them. It is worth noting that people of very high spiritual development almost always insist on checking with friends or spiritual advisers about the guidance they feel they have received from God."[2]

Morton Kelsey, an Episcopal priest, author and coun-
selor, tells how the practice of listening to God began for
him. Early in his career, he complained to a friend and
adviser, a practicing psychologist, that he wasn't getting
enough sleep and felt awful. He said he was in the habit
of waking up at 2 or 3 in the morning and then tossing
and turning until daybreak.

"The reason you can't sleep," said his friend, "is that
God wants to talk with you." Coming from a psychologist,
this was insulting to Kelsey who reminded his friend that
he himself knew something about God. His friend replied:
"This is the way God got in touch with Samuel. Do you
think He's changed?"

Kelsey said, "If we are hurting enough and someone
offers a sensible reason for some action, we will even do
something that seems as foolish to the world as getting up
in the middle of the night and trying to talk to God. I did
get up that night, and something spoke back that assured
me of love and concern and pointed to a way of courage
and discipline. After my half hour, I went back to bed and
went to sleep. I have continued this practice five or six
times each and every week over the last thirty years. This
practice, more than any other, has been the source of my
contact with a cosmic carer, the source of the thread that
has led me through the mazes I constantly keep falling
into. This time of quiet has been the source of the best
insights and inspirations and ideas that have come to me
over the years."[3]

Speaking to a group of judges and lawyers in Atlanta,
Bremer Hofmeyr of South Africa, a member of a promi-
nent Afrikaner family and a Rhodes Scholar at Oxford,
told of the difficulty of finding peaceful solutions to the
conflicts between African peoples, which he attributed to
a failure to seek God's will.

"Through working in many countries, among many cultures and many faiths, I have become convinced that in
every person who treads this earth there is in his make-
up as a human being the capacity to receive direction from
his Creator. I have also found this to be a most powerful

bond between seekers in the various faiths. This is a common experience we can share — possibly it is what makes us all human."[4]

Listening for the voice of our Creator may be a trait that makes us human, but it's obvious that all too few of us do it. This is too bad, for it's one of the ways in which we can practice turning our lives over to the care of God. To listen and to act on what we hear is to relinquish our will.

As we do this day by day, it becomes more natural for us to ask for guidance and to listen for the answer. We have to listen carefully to hear the answer. Often we must think long and hard about what we hear to make sure we understand it. We won't always know what we've heard. It'll make no sense to us. So we have to be patient.

Our answer may be just an impression of rightness about something or a feeling of confidence. We may suddenly understand something that had been baffling us and at the same time feel a spiritual connection. It may come in the form of a sudden welling up of joy within or a feeling of deep calm and well-being.

On the other hand, the lack of an answer may be a negative response or a signal to wait. God's way of getting through to us takes getting used to. There are no roadmaps in this spiritual territory, but we can explore with confidence. After all, there's no harm in listening.

Sometimes we have to just close our ears to the clamorings of our ego and open them to the still small voice of our Higher Power. The promptings of the spirit are like the whisper of a gentle breeze. We have to listen with rapt attention in order to make it out.

When we do hear something that seems filled with special meaning, then what? How do we know it's not our ego telling us what we want to hear? Buchman and Wright attributed a "luminous" quality to the thoughts that they believed came from God. Not everyone experiences the same thing. Still, we have to learn to trust ourselves. We will come to "know" the thoughts that stand out from the others. As they drift by, we suddenly realize there's one we want to take a look at. Then another catches our eye or ear or whatever receptor it is that snags passing thoughts.

Eventually we come to see that it's not so much a matter of standing guard with a butterfly net as it is just being present. We don't have to stalk the thoughts that count. As they go flitting by, often they'll land on our shoulder or brush our face with a gossamer wing. In one way or another, they make themselves known. Sooner or later we discover that just as we are after God, God is after us.

12

Practicing The Presence

· · · · · ·

The consciousness of God's presence
is the first principle of
religion.

— Hebrew Proverb

A lay brother with the seventeenth century barefooted Carmelite monks in Paris has become the model of attentiveness to God. Known as Brother Lawrence, he became the group's cook. There among his pots and pans, Brother Lawrence developed what he called the "practice of the presence of God" to such an extent that he claimed a sustained awareness, a sense of being upheld and guided through all of his activities, no matter how distracting they were.

"The time of business does not with me differ from the time of prayer," said Brother Lawrence. "And in the noise and clatter of my kitchen, while several persons are at the same time calling for different things, I possess God in as great tranquility as if I were upon my knees at the blessed sacrament."[1]

In our often frantically busy lives three hundred and some years later, it's hard to imagine being able to sustain an awareness of the presence of God for more than a few minutes at a time, let alone throughout the day. Besides, few of us are monks. Our lives aren't built around penance and prayer. Few of us have the time or even the inclination to devote all our waking moments to being aware of God.

But what if we did? What if we got in touch with our higher consciousness as soon as we awoke and asked for help? What if our singleminded purpose throughout the day was staying focused on God's will for us?

We do not need to be in monkish surroundings to hold our thoughts up to standards of love, honesty, purity and unselfishness. We do not need to be in a monastery to consider if we are being friendly, fair, helpful and forgiving. Many of us believe these to be attributes of God. If we think these things and do these things, aren't we practicing God's presence? Isn't it possible to do these things in all our activities and with everyone in our lives?

We are practicing the presence of God simply by being with the people we draw strength from in this program. And with others too, of course. There is no one we can't learn from, no one who in some way doesn't bring us something from God. If we are children of God, His creation, then there are divine attributes in each of us. So we need to pay careful attention to each other.

Silent prayer and meditation are useful for spiritual growth. All of us at one time or another need to, as the psalmist reported, "Be still and know that I am God." But few of us can spend our lives alone in quiet contemplation. We are social creatures. Not only is lengthy solitude unnatural and impractical, but for most people, it isn't healthy. It *is* healthy to be with people. It's healthy to listen and learn, trust and forgive. And to listen to what we ourselves are like as others reflect us. We have no better opportunity to practice the presence of God than to be in the presence of the people with whom we live and work and play.

In a profound sense, we are all brothers and sisters. We all share tender feelings of love and understanding. We are touched by God through each other. Someone reveals a personal weakness or triumph and we suddenly recognize ourselves — and in that instant feel a sort of universal kinship. Someone else says something uncharacteristically loving or does a purely unselfish thing, and it reaches the deepest core of our being. Suddenly we feel ourselves to be in the electric presence of the eternal. It's a sensation that doesn't lend itself to words. There's a sense of oneness, and then it's gone. But we know we were touched by the Almighty.

Whether we think so or not, or want to be or not, we are all transmitters of divine energy. Practicing fellowship — being attentive, concerned, caring and helpful to one another — is practicing the presence of God. That's not so hard because doing these things is at the very heart of our program.

Someone at an AA meeting said, "I came to this program to save my ass and found out it was attached to my soul."

The soul-felt presence of a loving God is one of the things we get from the 12 Steps. It's what makes the program work. And what saves our hide, day by day.

Staying God Conscious

Actually, the idea of practicing the presence of God is something of a paradox. God, of course, is everywhere. That must be true if God is God. We are always in God's presence. It's unavoidable. But to feel lonely and alienated from God is also unavoidable if we are human. We have all experienced the feeling of separation, what some have called the dark night of the soul. It's part of the human condition.

Our purpose on earth is known only to God, but it seems possible that one aspect of that purpose, one function, is to break out of the emotional prisons we've made for ourselves and return to our Creator. That doesn't come easily. Most of us are too ego driven to believe we need a Higher Power at all. It is when our lives are not working, when troubles pile up and become oppressive and frightening, that we realize maybe for the thousandth time that we could use some help after all. But as soon as things smooth out, with a nod to HP, we are off again on our lonely journey through fantasyland. The moments in which we sense God's reality are few and too far between. But by practice we can increase them and bring them closer together.

It is precisely as often as we can remember to practice the *presence* of God that we are successful in turning our will and our lives over to the *care* of God. It is precisely the success we have in lengthening the periods of consciousness of God's presence and shortening the intervals between, that we are able to leave our will and our lives in God's hands.

This practicing doesn't come naturally. It goes against the grain so we resist it. We are not used to opening our consciousness to an unseen and usually unfelt presence. But once felt we are apt to find this guiding presence so comforting that we return to the task, like it or not.

We can go to God in prayer, we can cultivate a receptive attitude in meditation, we can listen for God's guidance in quiet moments, but these are come-and-go propositions until we are able to remain on the same wavelength.

Becoming conscious of God's presence and cultivating that consciousness until it feels natural is probably the single most important thing we can do to keep from taking our will back once we've turned it over.

13

Climbing Jacob's Ladder

. . . . . .

*Once we have placed the key of
willingness in the lock and have the door
ever so slightly open, we find that we
can always open it some more.*

— Bill W.

racticing the presence of God makes us more inclined to turn our will over to the care of God, but it makes us no less human. As we sense God's presence, our physical needs and wants nevertheless keep poking us in the ribs, crying for attention, and some of our most selfish personality traits insist on expression. It's the ego's reaction, once again, to the threat of losing control. We identify so strongly with our selfish traits that it's hard to think of doing without them.

Unfortunately, we can't turn over to God something we aren't willing to let go of. Willingness is the key. Are we being honest with ourselves? Are we serious about being willing to turn *everything* over?

The words "our lives and our will" cover just about all there is. Once we've turned them over, we don't have much left to dicker with. Or do we? How many of us say we've turned our will and our lives over to the care of God while holding on to habits and character traits that we'd just as soon not even admit we have? Is there anyone who can truthfully say everything has been willingly given over to God? Are we harboring a secret resentment, a secret vice? Are we trying to ignore our conscience?

The Tale Of The Ladder

After I had been in the program a few months, I decided to use some of the extra time my newfound sobriety gave me to become a weekend handyman. Because I had spent almost all my spare time in bars or at home huddled over a hangover, there were a lot of jobs around the house that needed doing. For instance, the house needed a paint job. So one sober day I found myself in a self-service hardware store looking for an aluminum ladder. I found one that was suitable and affordable, then noticed a sturdier, more versatile model with no price tag on it. I surreptitiously peeled the sticker from the affordable ladder, stuck it on the other one and walked it through the checkout station, saving myself at least thirty dollars.

I didn't tell my sponsor about this little act of deceit, and I didn't seriously consider taking the ladder back even after personal honesty became important to me in working my program. But I never forgot it. As the years went by, I thought of it every now and then, usually when there was an occasion to use the ladder. I also thought of it in my weekly Step meeting, whenever the discussion turned to the Eighth and Ninth Steps that are concerned with making amends to people we have harmed. It bothered me. Just a little. An act of dishonesty had not been rectified. I had not made amends. As the years piled up, it became increasingly hard to see how trying to make amends so long after the act could do any good. The old hardware store was no longer there. The company, a nationwide chain, had built another one in a different part of town. The original store manager and clerks were nowhere to be found. Why not just forget it?

But I couldn't. I was trying to be honest and forthright in my dealings with people, and this reminded me of how far short of the mark I was, particularly since I had allowed it to go unresolved. There had been other acts of dishonesty over the years, things I liked to think of as small and unimportant. But the size of an offense is subjective. The person on the other end might see it differently. I knew this when I stopped to think about it, so I chose not to think about it often. Most of these offenses I had forgotten, but the lifted ladder kept coming to mind. It was sort of a symbol of all the other things that had troubled my conscience. It kept reminding me of my unwillingness to "go to any lengths."

I realized, at least subconsciously, that until I faced up to the incident of the ladder, I was not willing to turn my will over to God. Finally after an Eighth Step meeting one night, I became willing to make amends. I thought that if I was ever to have self-respect, I would have to make it right. So as soon as I cashed my paycheck that week I took a $50 bill and went to see the manager of the new hardware store. I nervously handed her the money and told her what had happened 15 years before. I said I had to make amends for cheating her company out of the money.

The manager was astounded. "What am I supposed to do with this?" she demanded. "I have no way of accounting for it."

She seemed offended yet was in awe of such audacious honesty.

"I don't get it," she said. "Why, after all these years, are you doing this?"

"I'm trying to live a different kind of life now," I explained. "Maybe the fifty will help cover a shortage. Or maybe one of your employees is in a bind and needs some money. You use it anyway you see fit. I took it from this company and this is where I have to make amends. Sorry if it causes a problem."

I walked out feeling somewhat lighter on my feet. My conscience was clear. It felt good. I had done another Ninth Step, while making a recommitment to the Third. I had demonstrated my willingness to turn it all over. This was something of a turning point. From here on out I thought there was a good chance I'd be more honest. I felt there was nothing I wouldn't be able to give up — or at least own up to — in the future.

Dishonesty blocks communication with my Higher Power. It's the spiritual equivalent of radio static and television snow. It's the same with all of our secrets — fears, resentments, petty conceits, lies, regrets, disappointments. If these are in focus, God is not.

I don't kid myself. I'm no saint. Spiritual progress comes slowly to me. I haven't got rid of my all-too-human pettiness just by righting a wrong. I can't expect to have my Creator on my mental screen all the time, in or out of focus. But the incident of the ladder helped me to see how spiritual blocks can alienate me from God.

When I'm feeling sorry for myself for any number of reasons — fear, anger, envy, confusion, rejection, whatever — I'm out of tune with my Higher Power. But I don't have to hang on to a spiritual block. I can do something about it. I can make an instant decision not to live with this obstacle to peace. I can turn it over.

Maybe tomorrow I'll be nursing a grudge. Maybe there'll be an injustice I can't forget. Someone spreading malicious tales. A fellow worker getting credit for something that I accomplished. Maybe I'll go out of my way to be nice to someone and not even get an acknowledgment. Or something worse.

It happens to all of us. For one reason or another — and life is full of these reasons — we're mad as hell. We can't figure out where God is in all this mental turmoil. Why isn't God helping us? We don't understand why we can't even seem to make contact.

Is it because our mind isn't really fixed on finding God's will? Maybe we're too busy nursing our emotional wounds. Instead of turning them over, we struggle with them, looking for our own answers. We look for them in all the wrong places, wondering where we went wrong, why we are being mistreated and how we can get even. In short, we turn to our ego instead of to God.

It should be clear to us by now that if our ego could supply the answers, we wouldn't still be hurting. We would already have done what's needed to heal the wounds and to find a solution to the troubling situation. We don't know the answers. We only think we do. That's precisely why we need to turn it over to God. All of it.

Although a number of spiteful things may come to mind, we don't know what to do about the people who have hurt us. So why not turn *them* over to God? We can't always control hurt feelings and there's no use fighting them. That only intensifies them. But we can make a decision, right now, to turn our feelings over to God, the one who *does* know how to deal with them.

All we really need is the willingness to be rid of whatever is blocking our spiritual progress — willingness to let go and let God.

14

Top Priority

. . . . . .

First things first.

— A saying posted on walls of
12-Step meeting rooms.

L ast of all, turning it over means putting our Higher Power first. It's a matter of survival. "Without help, it is too much for us. But there is One who has all power — that One is God."[1]

If we're smart, we put the One with the power first in our lives. But a lot of us tend to give our *feelings* a higher priority than God.

Well, somebody's bound to say, what's wrong with that? After all, aren't we in this program because we want to feel better? Sure, but feeling better is the by-product of a changed life, the result of practicing the principles of our program. No one ever achieved happiness by chasing it. Happiness hunts us down and claims us, though, once we have put first things first.

Our emotions are not something we can ignore, of course. They demand attention. Who of us is immune to feelings of fear, anger, confusion, frustration, helplessness or despair? Not many of us can handle them with equanimity. But God can deal with them for us and will if we just say the word, as countless people in our program can testify.

Getting My Priorities Straight

I worry too much about putting food on the table. But it shouldn't be my top priority. My boss is not the highest authority, although at times I act as if he is. I have to remind myself that my employer is someone with whom I have a contract to do a certain job, nothing more. If I can keep that in mind, I can work without fear. But if I see the boss as someone who controls my moods and can affect the course of my life, I have misplaced my priorities.

My job may be important to me for a variety of reasons. But holding onto it is not a life-or-death issue. It's not something for me to decide. It is my Higher Power's decision. Yet when I act as though keeping the job is all-important — that I must do so in order to support the family, pay the bills, maintain a certain lifestyle or whatever — then I am usurping the authority of my Higher Power.

I do, of course, want to perform to the best of my ability the work I'm hired to do. To do less is dishonest. But I have no reason to take the attitude that any job is crucial to my future happiness. God may have something more important and more fulfilling for me to do. So why worry?

When I worry about my future, I'm giving something else a higher priority than my Higher Power. Of all God's creatures, humans may be the only ones who do worry. We worry about money. We worry that we're not getting all the recognition that's due us. We worry that others are putting something over on us or treating us unfairly. We keep score. We wallow in resentment. We worry about our health. All needlessly. We can so easily turn our worries over. God welcomes them.

When we worry, we're giving something else a higher priority than our Higher Power.

How many other things do we assign a higher place on our scale of values? Does God take a back seat to money, possessions, sex, prestige, power? Even in our 12-Step groups, we occasionally see people playing politics, seeking to become known as outstanding speakers, setting themselves up as gurus and so on. When we spend a lot of time seeking approval from our companions, it may soothe our ego and massage our pride, but seldom does it bring us happiness. In fact, indulging in self-promotion and self-gratification to the exclusion of our spiritual growth always puts our recovery on hold and our serenity in jeopardy.

If we want security, peace of mind and smooth relationships with family, friends and fellow workers, the inner person has to change. And the kind of change that can achieve these goals depends not on self-discipline but on just the opposite — relinquishing control of ourselves and handing it over to our Higher Power.

Putting our Higher Power first doesn't ensure the disappearance of all our troubles but it enables us to accept whatever comes our way with grace and gratitude. It lets us experience happiness.

How can we *not* keep turning our will and our lives over to the care of a Higher Power who turns fear into confidence? Confusion into certainty? Anger into love?

God's love — what we obviously, urgently need above all else — is often low on our list of priorities. It's insane. Yet we go on resisting its call, day after day. We just can't believe that God's love, which we have long associated with weakness and sentimentality, can overcome something like anger, which we have long associated with strength and practicality.

We can't believe the power of God's love, so we give in to the demands of our ego. We embrace anger and fear. In doing so, we take back our will once more.

A story is told of a Hindu guru who took his disciple to the bank of a stream, grabbed his head and forced his face into the water, holding it submerged despite the frantic disciple's increasingly desperate struggles. Finally, with a mighty lunge, the disciple broke free and, noisily gasping for air, demanded "Why?"

"When you want Brahman (God) as much as you wanted air," said the guru, "you shall have Him."

We have always had God because God has always had us. But perhaps we have not turned our will and our lives entirely over because we have not wanted God as much as we want air.

God knows this is hard for us to do. That's why it doesn't have to be a now-or-never thing. We can make the decision repeatedly, every time an opportunity comes. If done often enough, it becomes a habit almost as natural as breathing and just as important.

 **Notes**

Chapter 1 — Center Of The Universe

1. **The Language of the Heart,** p. 236, *AA Grapevine*, NY, 1988.

Chapter 4 — Getting Your Feet Wet

1. Gregory Vlastos, *The Religious Way*, quoted in **The Choice Is Always Ours,** p. 56-57, ed. Elizabeth B. Howes, Harper & Row, 1989.

2. Bill W., **Twelve Steps and Twelve Traditions,** (gift edition, 15th printing) p. 40, Alcoholics Anonymous World Services, 1952, 1953, 1985.

3. *AA Grapevine*, September 1986, p. 11, Alcoholics Anonymous Grapevine, New York, NY, 1986.

Chapter 5 — The Chief Clown

1. *AA Grapevine*, December 1984, p. 32-34, Alcoholics Anonymous Grapevine, New York, NY, 1984.

Chapter 6 — The Jack-In-The-Box Connection

1. **A Course In Miracles,** Vol. One, p. 78, Foundation For Inner Peace, Tiburon, CA, 1976.

2. Ibid., Vol. Two, p. 48.

Chapter 7 — Negative Feedback

1. *AA Grapevine,* December 1981, p. 22, Alcoholics Anonymous Grapevine, New York, NY, 1981.

2. Bill W., **Twelve Steps and Twelve Traditions,** p. 90.

3. **A Course In Miracles,** Vol. One, p. 593.

Chapter 8 — Accentuate The Positive

1. The **Oxford Dictionary of Quotations.**

2. Mary McDermott Shideler, **In Search Of The Spirit,** p. 212, Ballantine, New York, NY, 1985.

3. *AA Grapevine,* April 1983, p. 16.

Chapter 9 — Look Who's Talking To God

1. Silvio E. Fittipaldi, **How to Pray Always (Without Always Praying),** p. 24, Liguori Publications, Liguori, MO, 1985.

2. Alexis Carrell, **Man, The Unknown,** p. 147, Harper, New York, NY, 1935.

3. Elie Wiesel, **Night,** Avon, New York, NY, 1969.

4. Fittipaldi, **How To Pray Always (Without Always Praying),** p. 20.

5. Edouard LeRoy, *Le Probleme de Dieu,* quoted in **The Choice Is Always Ours,** p. 209.

6. Donald G. Bloesch, **The Struggle Of Prayer,** p. 6, Helmers & Howard, Colorado Springs, CO, 1988.

7. **A Course In Miracles,** Vol. One, p. 585.

8. G.K. Chesterton, **Orthodoxy,** p. 68, Bodley Head, London, 1908.

9. Shideler, **In Search Of The Spirit,** p. 191.

10. Elizabeth Hunter, **The Choice Is Always Ours,** p. 285.

Chapter 10 — Tricking The Mind

1. **The Cloud Of Unknowing,** p. 53, trans. Ira Progoff, Dell Books, New York, NY, 1957.

2. *The AA Grapevine,* March 1985, p. 11.

3. Herbert Benson, **The Relaxation Response,** pp. 161-162, William Morrow, New York, NY, 1975.

4. William James, **The Varieties Of Religious Experience,** p. 367, American World Library, New York, NY, 1958.

5. *The AA Grapevine,* November, 1984, p. 28.

Chapter 11 — What's That I Hear?

1. Garth Lean, **On The Tail Of A Comet,** p. 74, Helmers & Howard, Colorado Springs, CO, 1988.

2. Bill W., **Twelve Steps and Twelve Traditions,** p. 60.

3. Morton T. Kelsey, **Companions On The Inner Way,** pp. 136-137, Crossroad, New York, NY, 1989.

4. Bremer Hofmeyr, *For A Change* Magazine, Good Road Ltd. London, UK, Nov. 1989.

Chapter 12 — Practicing The Presence

1. Brother Lawrence, **The God Illuminated Cookbook,** p. 59, Church Of The Way, East Ridge Press, Hankins, NY, 1975.

Chapter 14 — Top Priority

1. **Alcoholics Anonymous,** p. 59.

 # Bibliography

AA Grapevine, The International Monthly Journal of Alcoholics Anonymous, which presents the experiences and opinions of AA members and others, New York, NY.

A Course In Miracles, 1975, Foundation for Inner Peace, Tiburon, CA.

Alcoholics Anonymous, "The Big Book," the basic text for Alcoholics Anonymous, Third Edition, 1976, AA World Services, New York, NY.

Anonymous, **The Cloud Of Unknowing,** ed. Ira Progoff, 1957, Dell Books, New York, NY.

Benson, Herbert, **The Relaxation Response,** 1975, William Morrow, New York, NY.

Bloesch, Donald G., **The Struggle For Prayer,** 1988, Helmers & Howard, Colorado Springs, CO.

Brother Lawrence, **The Practice Of The Presence Of God,** 1895, Fleming H. Revell, New York, NY.

Carrell, Alexis, **Man, The Unknown,** 1935, Harper & Brothers, New York, NY.

Chesterton, G.K., **Orthodoxy,** 1908, The Bodley Head, London.

Fenelon, Francois, quoted in the anthology **The Choice Is Always Ours,** ed. Elizabeth Boyden Howes, 1989, Harper & Row, San Francisco, CA.

Fittipaldi, Silvio E., **How To Pray Always (Without Always Praying),** 1985, Liguori Publications, Liguori, MO.

Hofmeyr, Bremer, *For A Change* Magazine, 1989, Good Road, London.

Hunter, Elizabeth, **The Choice Is Always Ours,** ed. Elizabeth Boyden Howes, 1989, Harper & Row, San Francisco, CA.

James, William, **The Varieties Of Religious Experience,** Foreword, 1958, The New American Library of World Literature, New York, NY.

Kelsey, Morton T., **Companions On The Inner Way,** 1983, Crossroad Publishing, New York, NY.

The Language Of The Heart, 1988, Bill W.'s writings in *The AA Grapevine,* The AA Grapevine Inc., New York, NY.

Lean, Garth, **On The Tail Of A Comet,** 1988, Helmers & Howard, Colorado Springs, CO.

LeRoy, Edouard, *Le Probleme de Dieu,* quoted in **The Choice Is Always Ours,** 1989, ed. Elizabeth Boyden Howes, Harper & Row, San Francisco, CA.

The Oxford Dictionary of Quotations, Third Edition, 1979, Oxford and New York.

Pass It On, 1984, the story of Bill Wilson and how Alcoholics Anonymous came about, AA World Services, New York, NY.

Shideler, Mary McDermott, **In Search Of The Spirit,** 1985, Ballantine Books, New York, NY.

Vlastos, Gregory, *The Religious Way,* quoted in **The Choice Is Always Ours,** ed. Elizabeth Boyden Howes, 1989, Harper & Row, San Francisco, CA.

Wiesel, Elie, **Night,** 1969, Avon, New York, NY.

Wilson, Bill, **Twelve Steps And Twelve Traditions,** AA World Services, New York, NY.

Notes

Notes

Daily Affirmation Books from . . .
Health Communications

GENTLE REMINDERS FOR CO-DEPENDENTS: Daily Affirmations
Mitzi Chandler

With insight and humor, Mitzi Chandler takes the co-dependent and the
adult child through the year. Gentle Reminders is for those in recovery
who seek to enjoy the miracle each day brings.

ISBN 1-55874-020-1   **$6.95**

TIME FOR JOY: Daily Affirmations
Ruth Fishel

With quotations, thoughts and healing energizing affirmations these daily
messages address the fears and imperfections of being human, guiding us
through self-acceptance to a tangible peace and the place within where
there is *time for joy.*

ISBN 0-932194-82-6   **$6.95**

AFFIRMATIONS FOR THE INNER CHILD
Rokelle Lerner

This book contains powerful messages and helpful suggestions aimed at
adults who have unfinished childhood issues. By reading it daily we can
end the cycle of suffering and move from pain into recovery.

ISBN 1-55874-045-6   **$6.95**

DAILY AFFIRMATIONS: For Adult Children of Alcoholics
Rokelle Lerner

Affirmations are a way to discover personal awareness, growth and
spiritual potential, and self-regard. Reading this book gives us an
opportunity to nurture ourselves, learn who we are and what we want
to become.

ISBN 0-932194-47-3
(Little Red Book)   **$6.95**
(New Cover Edition)   **$6.95**

SOOTHING MOMENTS: Daily Meditations For Fast-Track Living
Bryan E. Robinson, Ph.D.

This is designed for those leading fast-paced and high-pressured lives
who need time out each day to bring self-renewal, joy and serenity into
their lives.

ISBN 1-55874-075-9   **$6.95**

3201 S.W. 15th Street,
Deerfield Beach, FL 33442-8190
1-800-851-9100

Health Communications, Inc.®

New Books . . .
from Health Communications

HEAL YOUR SELF-ESTEEM: Recovery From Addictive Thinking
Bryan Robinson, Ph.D.

Do you have low self-esteem? Do you blame others for your own unhappiness? If so, you may be an addictive thinker. The 10 Principles For Healing, an innovative, positive approach to recovery, are integrated into this book to provide a new attitude with simple techniques for recovery.

ISBN 1-55874-119-4 $9.95

HEALING ENERGY: The Power Of Recovery
Ruth Fishel, M.Ed., C.A.C.

Linking the newest medical discoveries in mind/body/spirit connections with the field of recovery, this book illustrates how to balance ourselves mentally, physically and spiritually to overcome our addictive behavior.

ISBN 1-55874-128-3 $9.95

CREDIT, CASH AND CO-DEPENDENCY: The Money Connection
Yvonne Kaye, Ph.D.

Co-dependents and Adult Children seem to experience more problems than most as money can be used as an anesthetic or fantasy. Yvonne Kaye writes of the particular problems the co-dependent has with money, sharing her own experiences.

ISBN 1-55874-133-X $9.95

THE LAUNDRY LIST: The ACoA Experience
Tony A. and Dan F.

Potentially The Big Book of ACoA, *The Laundry List* includes stories, history and helpful information for the Adult Child of an alcoholic. Tony A. discusses what it means to be an ACoA and what the self-help group can do for its members.

ISBN 1-55874-105-4 $9.95

LEARNING TO SAY NO: Establishing Healthy Boundaries
Carla Wills-Brandon, M.A.

If you grew up in a dysfunctional family, establishing boundaries is a difficult and risky decision. Where do you draw the line? Learn to recognize yourself as an individual who has the power to say no.

ISBN 1-55874-087-2 $8.95

3201 S.W. 15th Street,
Deerfield Beach, FL 33442-8190
1-800-441-5569

Health Communications, Inc.